W. H. Lever

Following the Flag

Jottings of a Jaunt Round the World

W. H. Lever

Following the Flag
Jottings of a Jaunt Round the World

ISBN/EAN: 9783337189778

Printed in Europe, USA, Canada, Australia, Japan

Cover: Foto ©Andreas Hilbeck / pixelio.de

More available books at **www.hansebooks.com**

Following the Flag

JOTTINGS OF A JAUNT ROU THE WORLD

W. H. LEVER

*WITH NUMEROUS ILLUSTRATIONS
FROM PHOTOGRAPHS*

LONDON

CONTENTS.

TORONTO
CHICAGO
SAN FRANCISCO
SANDWICH ISLANDS
HONOLULU
HABITS AND CUSTOMS
SANDWICH ISLANDS AND UNITED STATES
VOLCANO OF KILAUEA
VOLCANO OF HALEMOUMOU
SAMOA
ARRIVAL IN NEW ZEALAND
THE MAORIES AND THE LAND
WAPOLAPU
ERUPTION OF TARAWERA
NAPIER TO DUNEDIN
NEW ZEALAND'S LABOUR GOVERNMENT
GRADUATED LAND TAX
LABOUR LEGISLATION
AUSTRALIA
AUSTRALIAN DAIRY FARMING
SYDNEY AND BRISBANE
AUSTRALIA AND ONE MAN ONE VOTE
AUSTRALIA AND FREE TRADE
AUSTRALIA AND THE LAND QUESTION
AUSTRALIAN RAILWAYS AND FINANCE

INTRODUCTORY.

These Jottings are records of a Voyage round the W from September, 1892, to March, 1893, the route being thr Canada and the States to the Sandwich Islands, New Zea and Australia, and home by the Suez Canal.

The jottings originally appeared in the form of lette "The Birkenhead News," and the Illustrations are Photographs, some few of which were taken by the writer, the remainder purchased at the places to which they refer.

TORONTO.

INDIAN BABY.

ON the arrival of the "Germa[nic]" in New York we were deta[ined] by quarantine regulations for a[bout] twelve hours. This appeared t[o] all impatient passengers quite [use]less, seeing that there was n[o] solitary case of sickness of any [kind] on board, and that we had [been] practically quarantined on the Atl[antic] for nine long days. But we were [told] it was absolutely necessary fo[r the] sanitary authorities of New [York] to show how vigilant and careful they were, and that we h[ad to] be sacrificed to encourage implicit faith on the part o[f the] American public in the completeness of all the arrangements [made] by the medical officers for preventing the introduction of cho[lera].

We took a cab to the hotel, paying three do[llars] (12s. 6d.) for a distance for which we should pay 2[s. or] 2s. 6d. in England. This little incident reminds on[e of a] story. A certain well-known merchant from Liverpoo[l, a] tall, fine, dignified, and impressive man, a trifle pomp[ous] perhaps, and with a due idea of his own importance—o[n his] first arrival in New York, took a cab, and in time reache[d his] hotel. He looked out for the hotel porter to lift dow[n his] luggage, but none being forthcoming, he, with great dig[nity] reached his belongings down himself, the driver not [offer]ing the slightest assistance. "Driver, what is your fa[re?]" "Four dollars" "Are you sure that is your right fa[re?]" "No, I ain't; my fare is five dollars, but you looked su[ch a]

cause, he was so "bounced" that he paid the four dollar lamb, and carried his luggage into the hotel with a: dignity as the occasion was capable of. One can imagin a shock he must have suffered, and how strange and fortable everything would seem when he afterwards, in tl dining-room, called the waiter. Instead of the brisk sir," "Coming, sir," "Directly, sir," "Yes, sir; what get for you, sir?" accompanied by the hurrying eager oblige, to which we are accustomed at home, he would put up with the loitering, free-and-easy stroll across the r the American waiter, with his short "What do you want generally indifferent way of doing things.

The first great impression one receives on landing York is of the hurry and bustle of the place, the nervous the vitality and force of the American people, and th speed at which buildings there are being put up. succeeding visit, however short the interval, one note changes in the appearance of every American city.

During our stay at Toronto we were told that we to hear one of their celebrated preachers who had a great popularity. We went, and could hardly believe t were attending a religious service on a Sunday morning. thing was conducted in so entirely different a manner t we are accustomed to in England. Perhaps we are slow in these matters, but it did seem to me that in this lar instance our older fashioned way was the best. audience—or I suppose I ought rather to say the co tion -applauded whenever the Minister said anythin particularly appealed to them, and as this occurred v quently, there was a constant clapping of hands and stan feet. The Sunday morning on which we were there happ be the occasion of their annual collection in aid of the n and the collection was made just before the sermon beg minister announcing it in the following words: "Well, Sunday in October is here at last, and a long time it has coming, that is, to some of us. (Laughter.) Well, it

boys, go ahead with the boxes." During the collection a y[oung?]
of about sixteen played a cornet solo; and, when he had finis[hed]
the minister turned round to him and said, "Well, boy,
strum pretty well on that instrument. Another day, mind
come right here to the front; you are a good-looking boy,
we want to see you." In the same way, in reading the chap[ter]
out of the Bible, he made running comments, reducing the s[itua]
tion to parallels with every-day nineteenth century life in a [way]
that was not agreeable to listen to, especially when every
and then these flying remarks called forth clapping of hands
stamping of feet.

At night we went to the English Church Cathedral, an[d as]
you would expect, we found the church that was neither e[stab]
lished nor endowed by the State to be robust, vigorous,
filled to overflowing. We had the pleasure of hearing a g[ood]
hearty, sermon. The preacher, the Reverend Canon Dumo[ulin]
took for his subject, "My people." He pointed out [that]
however radical or democratic a man might be, he was n[ot so]
radical or democratic as the Bible, or as the church and reli[gion]
when founded on the Bible; that religion and the church [are]
of the people, for the people, by the people; that all co[ntrol]
must be in the hands of the people, not in the hands of e[ither]
State or clergy, or beyond the direct control of the people. [He]
also said that in thirty out of the thirty-seven churche[s in]
Toronto, the seats were entirely free, and that the worship[pers]
could sit in any seat they found vacant; also that they hope[d to]
make the remainder free in a very short time. He ma[de a]
strong comparison between this state of affairs and the e[xclu]
siveness of the dissenting churches and chapels of Toront[o, in]
which he said certain pews were appropriated by certain wor[ship]
pers, thus encouraging exclusiveness and doing away with [the]
equality amongst the worshippers that ought to exist. This [was]
a hard hit, and I agreed that it was a well-deserved one, l[but I]
had to rub my eyes to see whether we were really in the Tor[onto]
Cathedral of the English Church, or at some Radical mee[ting.]
If a dis-established and dis-endowed church can be so st[rong]
and robust, so in touch with the life of the people, so oppos[ed]

people or suffer loss in any way on that account. Shoul[d]
ever happen, it will be Dissenters of all denomination[s]
will require to broaden their ideas that they may not su[ffer]
the change, or be in danger of losing the hold they now p[ossess].

Everywhere in Canada and the States one finds ele[ctricity]
and the electric light developed far beyond what we see in [every]
day life in England. The tramcars in almost all the cit[ies are]
driven by electricity. The houses, shops, and streets are l[ighted]
by the same means. I have seen lighted by electricity ev[en the]
smallest shops, of the class we call in England "toffy s[hops"]
—that is, shops with a bottle of sweets, a piece of bathbri[ck and]
two pipes crossed in the window.

CHICAGO.

WE spent a few days in Chicago, visiting the World's and as far as one could judge in its present incom[plete] state, the Americans have every cause to feel proud of this m[onu]ment of their energy. For picturesqueness of situation, b[eauty] and extent of buildings, **arrangement**, conception, and ge[neral] execution, it leaves nothing to be desired, and ough[t to] be the finest Exhibition the world has ever seen. The [site] is unique, extending over 700 acres of park land on [the] shores of that beautiful inland sea, Lake Michigan. [The] dimensions of the buildings are proportionate to this enor[mous] area, the ground covered by the main building alone being [over] 40 acres, and the total area covered by all the buildings [being] over 200 acres. In addition to size, which of itself is al[ways] impressive, each building, from a purely architectural po[int of] view, is well conceived, duly proportioned, and most admi[rably] executed.

As is well-known, Chicago is increasing her popul[ation] literally by leaps and bounds, and she aspires shortly to oc[cupy] the foremost position in this respect in the United St[ates,] surpassing even New York herself. Geographically, Chi[cago] occupies a fine position, which makes her naturally the c[apital] of the North-west. One cannot help being impressed wit[h the] great speed at which the people are living. All is one perp[etual] drive, without cessation or rest. Business and pleasure, S[unday] and week day, appear to be all the same. You notice at [once] the drawn, haggard, prematurely old faces of the work girl[s and] youths going to the offices and stores each morning. They [look] more wearied and tired than they ought to when leaving [their] work at night. Compare them with the bright, healthy [look]

the exact opposite of this condition strikes the observer.]
of no city where the work girls and youths appear so brigh
move with so buoyant a step, as in Toronto. I am very
mistaken if the "sweater" has not got a firm grip in Cl
and it would not take much to convince me that, he
much of a paradise it may be for the capitalist, it is the
opposite for the workers.

Another city which has made great and rapid growth
Lake City. The progress there is simply wonderful. E
cars, electric lights, enormous stone buildings, costly]
are there. In fact, it appears to have sprung from ra
sleepy village into a brisk, busy city since my first visi
four years ago. The Gentiles claim all the credit for this.
advent was opposed by the Mormons, who no doubt sa
their own power and influence would cease to exist
the altered conditions the Gentiles would bring with
Mormonism, in fact, is fast dying out. Free schools are
started, and with better education it is not possible th
rising generation will place themselves, as in the old
their fathers did before them, under the control of
prophet, apostles, or deacons. These high priests collect
per cent. of the earnings of every man, woman, and chil
in addition arrogated to themselves the right to interf
every affair of life, even to dictating how many wives a
ought to marry. It is not generally known, but it was or
consent of these high priests that the Mormon was allow
marry more than one wife, and not only so, but he was o
to marry additional wives at their command. Of c
education was not encouraged. It was only over the ig
that such power could be held. I suppose it never w
known what enormous sums of money the Mormons col
by their titheings, or what has become of the same. A
present moment suits are pending in the American c
between the children of Brigham Young and the Mc
Church, to determine who is entitled to the three or four m
left by that clever impostor, for that he was an impostor the

lifetime and went lecturing throughout the country aga
both himself and Mormonism. His favourite wife, Am
married again after his death, although, he being a prophe
was not lawful according to the Mormon law for her to do
However, Brigham Young rests peacefully enough now,
from all his domestic worries, in his own secluded burial gro
in which each wife has her little burial plot marked out for
in rotation next to the Prophet's, according to the priorit

THE GATES AJAR.

their marriage. Each wife, that is, except the two faitl
ones. As the wives are not dying in the order in which
were married, that little burial ground presents a bro
appearance. You can tell exactly which wives have still to
to complete the arrangement and make Brigham Young's bi
plot complete. The children, I understand—and there 1
some 80 of them—are not to be buried in this plot. Prob
they will require ultimately a whole cemetery to themsel
their wives and families, or perhaps a county will be spec
reserved as a cemetery for them. When I asked what

population of 50,000, 5,000 Sunday school children wa[lk in]
one procession on Columbus Day.

Whilst at Salt Lake City we visited the barracks [of]
Indian soldiers. The United States Government is try[ing to]
train to some useful purpose, but I understand with ver[y little]
success. The "noble red man" will not work, and is t[oo proud]
to become a soldier. The Government is continually [taking]
away his "reservation" hunting grounds, and therefor[e must]
keep him in idleness or let him starve. Each year s[ees the]
poor Indian driven out of some spot he had formerly oc[cupied,]
and as there are still about 200,000 Indians in the [United]
States, it has become a serious problem to know what [to do]
with them; and no doubt the Government thinks that it [would]
be an easy way out of the difficulty if only these Indians [could]
be trained to make good and efficient soldiers.

The Americans are more expert than ourselves in th[e art]
of gardening known as "carpet bedding," and we s[aw at]
Golden Gate Park, San Francisco, and at most of th[e]

novelties we saw were at Chicago, in Washington Park. T
the gardeners had cleverly seized on the most exciting
of the day (the Presidential Election), and had produced a n
of a race between two canoes, the occupant of one represe
General Harrison; the other, Grover Cleveland. The
canoes and canoeists—each with paddle—were entirely
posed of flowers and foliage plants. The figures of Har
and Cleveland were tolerably life-like, with eyes, nose, m
ears, coat, waistcoat, and hat, complete even to collars and
The goal, which was represented by an imitation of the I
dential chair, was placed at a point both boats were appar
making for. This chair was wonderfully realistic, with a
cushion carelessly placed on the seat. For some time we tho

PRESIDENTIAL RACE.

that at any rate the cushion was a cloth one, but it was
like everything else, it was the result of the gardeners' skill
doubt it is all composed on a frame-work of wood, covered
wire netting, packed with moss and peaty soil in which
plants are placed. In another part of this park there

complete. There are also the calendar, which is altere
day ; sundials ; flags of all nations ; graceful vases, etc.,
built up in plants and flowers, and all looking real and
These novelties make the American parks a great attr
and bring crowds of city people to view them. Our
parks in England suffer greatly from want of novelty, a

SUN DIAL.

gardeners, if provided with the means, could, according
season, produce as great a variety of designs. The aim
be to introduce as often as possible something fresh and
something that would draw the public to the park, into th
air and away from the streets and slums.

SAN FRANCISCO.

WHILST we were in San Francisco we heard more plaints of trade and business generally than at any place we visited in the States. California is not, and pro never can become, a manufacturing state, bu can and does raise enormous crops of fruit, w and grapes, out of which latter large quantit wine are made. Some fruit is sent by tra

CHINESE FRUIT PEDLAR.

the Eastern States, but Florida, being better placed fo market, is a strong competitor. The bulk of the wi

of the world. But in the meantime the bulk of the profit find their way into the pockets of the middleman or b and not into the pockets of the grower.

A visit to San Francisco would not be complete withou to China Town. Here the Chinese have set up their theatr houses, and opium dens, and herd and crowd together in that would kill the European right off. On the Chinese, ho

STREET, CHINA TOWN.

it appears to h effect; they ar smooth, well n ed, and h enough, and p have just as contempt for can ways of li Americans ca sibly have for Their sleek, satisfied, and c ed look say anyhow. Wh sees their wo industry, vitali quiet persisten it is not hard to that they are d to play a ve portant part future history world. No E man preserv national habi dress, religio thought, and Fatherland so unaffected by other nations as does the Chi If the Chinaman were as warlike and pugnacious as the E

SAN FRANCISCO.

China Town, which is conducted, as are mai
institutions. on a system exactly the opposite of
for whilst we pay someone to conduct our re

the Chinese, on the other hand, put up for tender each ye
privilege of conducting theirs. Last year the price paid fo
right for this Temple was 5,500 dollars, but it did not prove a
speculation. Consequently, this year the highest tender wa
5,000 dollars. I understand that there is a fixed scale of ch
for whatever the worshippers want, in the way of special off
and supplications to the idols, so that we may take
granted that this fall in price points to fewer occasio
invoking the favour of the idols, such as births, marr
deaths, good luck or bad luck, etc. There
special idol set up in all these temples fo
gamblers, and we are told that this idol re
more offerings than all the others put together.
all their idols, he is supposed at one time t
lived on earth. He is repres
as dressed in rough sackclo
the very depths of povert
first it seemed in cong
that gamblers should
worship an idol whose
power over luck was
no greater than this.
It should hardly take
the skill of their idol
to get down to sack-
cloth. But on inquiry
we were inform-
ed that the idol
is represented
as he once lived
in the depths
of poverty, and
that afterwards
he won untold
riches and be-
came powerful

CHINESE LADY

SAN FRANCISCO.

FOLLOWING THE FLAG.

greater than any of his followers could be called upon to [...] would not appeal with force to the human heart.

We next paid a visit to the Chinese theatre, where the p[...] that was "running" was a comparatively short one, as it wo[...] only take about two months to get through. Usually, a Chi[...] piece takes three or four months, of six hours each night. T[...] follow the hero from the cradle to the grave, and don't hurry [...] All the characters are taken by men—women are not allowed to act—and men who can successfully take female parts command high salaries. The actors usually live under the theatre, in very little hovels or boxes, about six feet by five feet, without daylight or ventilation, and as we visited these we had an opportunity of seeing the home life of the actors. Some few are married. In one of these rabbit hutches the wife was quietly sewing, and her little child, a girl of about seven or eight, sang us a few missionary songs — she attended the American Mission School—and then one or two Chinese songs. At the close of her performance, the little lady shook hands all round, and said "How do you do?" "Glad to see you," "Come again soon," in broken English. Small as these dens are, in several we saw that the occupiers were entertaining their friends with opium smoking, card playing, or some form of gambling. In one we were shown the principal actor of female parts, who is paid the comparati[...] high salary of 2,500 dollars a year. We noticed his lo[...] delicate, tapered fingers and his youthful face, and could [...] understand that, as no doubt his voice would suit a wom[...]

are never changed. A board hung prominently in the f
describes what the scene is intended to represent, and
have to imagine that you see trees, houses, battlefi
interiors, or exteriors, as the case may be. All through
acting there is a never ceasing din of gongs, tom toms,
just as if the main object of the orchestra was to drown
voices of the actors.

We next visited the various opium dens and numerous c
sights, finishing by taking a cup of tea at a Chinese res
rant. We did not feel equal to making an attempt on
" birds' nest " soup, " sharks' fins," " roast puppy," and c
delicacies that can be had there. The restaurant was the fasl
able one of China Town. The fittings and woodwork wer
made in China, brought over, and fixed in the true Chi
fashion.

SANDWICH ISLANDS.

WE sailed by S.S. "Australia" from San Francisco on 26th October, in beautiful weather, and with a steady refreshing breeze. The sea is a deep ultramarine

Henry Moore's sea paintings was overdone, but here we
just that deep blue he knows so well how to paint. W
plenty of flying fish. The gulls here are enormous black fe
almost twice the size of our own gulls. They skim again
wind without even the flutter of a wing just as easily as
do with the wind. The temperature in the shade varies
seventy-five to eighty degrees, and as the deck is co
with an awning, under which there is always a cool, refre
breeze, the voyage becomes the perfection of ocean t
The meals are early, 5.30 being the last at night, so
"early to bed and early to rise" is a rule imposed (
by necessity. We are looking forward with all eage
to Honolulu and the Sandwich Islands, with their won(
volcanoes, said to be the largest and grandest in the worl

Travelling in the Sandwich Islands is quite easy. The isla
have adopted European methods, and also even our for
government. If Captain Cook returned he certainly \
not know the place nor the habits and customs of the na
for now-a-days instead of settling the question of the g(
ment by a "Battle Royal," followed by a banquet fo
victors, with "Long Pig" (cannibal style) for the prir
dish, the Islanders adopt the comparatively peaceful
unpicturesque ballot box, with election addresses, caucuses
all the modern "improvements." But somehow, in spite (
blessings of civilisation, it happens that whilst in Ca
Cook's day the population of the Islands was 400,000, n
barely reaches 90,000, of whom only 35,000 are na
How shall we judge which is best for the natives—which
fulfils the doctrine of the "greatest good of the gr(
number"?

The eighteen days we passed on the Sandwich Is
will always be a happy memory. It was our first exper
of tropical scenery and tropical luxuriance of veget:
When one sees for the first time rare tropical p
such as in England are reared with difficulty in hot-hc
growing in wild profusion in cottage gardens, in the (

coffee and sugar plantations, that curious looking cactus th[at] bears the fruit called "prickly pear," mangoes, dates, papay[a,] pomegranates, tamarinds, and tree ferns, to say nothing of fie[lds] of rice, all give to the country a strange and foreign appearan[ce] that tells us plainly and unmistakably how far we are from hor[ne.] Yet, notwithstanding all this luxuriant beauty, we do not fi[nd]

HONOLULU.

that it rivals that of our own country. When once the novelty [of] these pretty scenes has passed away, we reflect that the maje[sty] of the oak or the elm far and away surpasses that of the palm tr[ee,] that a field of wheat is more beautiful in its waving grace than [a] field of sugar cane, that a field of turnips, although it may [not] appeal so strongly to the imagination and fancy, is brighter a[nd] fresher to look at than a field of pineapples, and, not least of [all,] that our English meadows and hedges have a charm that the ba[re] looking, yellow, dried-up lands of the tropics can in no w[ay] approach.

We arrived at Honolulu November 2nd, and on looking ba[ck] we are surprised to recall how vague and undefined were our id[eas] of the place. We had the impression, probably like most others

advanced views for a "native," and as a man who was ⟨
to introduce "white" government into his realm. W
imagined a city such as we found Honolulu to be, wit
fine avenues and streets most thoroughly and perfectly
by electricity, with a complete and extensive tramway
with telephones in every business house and most of the
residences, and with Royal Palace, Government Buildir
Parliament. We found there every sign of modern civi
even that latest product of the culture of the age, "1
boom-de-ay," and after we heard it yelled by a Sou
Islander's child we were prepared for anything an
surprised at nothing.

At first in Honolulu we felt the heat very much. The
meter registered 80° in the shade during the day and un
10 o'clock at night, and all the time we were there we or
saw it fall below 75° day or night. On the other hand,
rose above 82°, and I believe this is the usual experience
round. The cool "trade winds" blow here for nine mo
the year, and consequently after we got over the first fe
and had changed to cooler clothing, we felt no inconv
from tl
and for
and se
ing the
is sim
l i g h
E n e r
work,h
especia
"white
is not p
I do no
that v
i m p o
but or

DRAINAUD HEAD FROM WAIKIKI.

energetic, determined, hard work is impossible. A H

SANDWICH ISLANDS.

slipped by, simply because the exertion of doing so appea[rs]
such a burden and labour that he shrank from undertaking [it].
This exactly illustrates the feeling one has out here. Ther[e is]
no energy or eagerness, and the most trivial task appe[ars]
a mountain of labour.

The great delight here is sea bathing. It is indul[ged]
in by everyone at all hours of the day and night, and moonli[ght]

NATIVES SWIMMING, WAIKIKI.

bathing picnics are quite an institution. I am very fond of
bathing, and have bathed in many places, but certainly ne[ver]
knew what sea bathing was until I bathed at Honolulu
Waikiki Bay. A beautiful sandy beach, enclosed within a c[oral]
reef, which effectually keeps out sharks, a gentle rolling s[urf,]
and water which is beautifully blue and clear, of a temperat[ure]
varying between 75° and 80°, make sea bathing at Waikiki

provide themselves with flat boards of a length and
varying according to taste. Armed with this they
out to just that point of the breakers where the waves
to curl over, and choosing a large one dexterously
themselves in front and on the top of it, and are carried a
speed high up on the beach. Occasionally one of the surf
will miss the exact time to catch the wave and is consec
left behind or tumbled over amidst the laughter and sh
the others. To onlookers the sport appears very simple an
but in reality it is not so. Great skill and practice are ne
hit off the exact time and point at which to mount the br
to be either too soon or too late is fatal to success. The ex
tion and excitement this sport affords to those who take
it reminds one most forcibly of the fun of toboggan
Canada.

HONOLULU.

HONOLULU has a population of some 23,000, and suppo[rts] one morning daily paper, one evening daily, and seve[ral] weeklies, besides periodicals, but having no cable connecti[on] with the outside world, or even with the other islands of the grou[p] and having only a bi-monthly mail service, it is not difficult [to] understand that the editor must find it almost impossible to p[ro]vide news fresh each day for his readers. The following ite[m] which was given a prominent position in the daily summary copied out of the Honolulu morning paper :—" Work on t[he] new warehouse for W. G. Irwin and Co. has been stopped [for] the present, the contractor having exhausted his supply [of] bricks." It is clear that the editor had exhausted his supply [of] news. This was followed a few days later by a paragra[ph] announcing that, the contractor having received a fresh supply of bricks, building operations had been renewed. All this sounds very absurd to us; but if we imagine a city of only 23,000 inhabitants, separated by water from the rest of the world, with no tele-

PRISONERS.

be possible. Not only are the prisoners employed i
making, but they are actually hired out at 50 cents a
whoever wishes to employ them. If citizens want the
of a "handy" man to mow the lawn or weed the
they can telephone to the Governor of the jail, and

PALM TREES IN PRIVATE GARDEN.

send up at
"felony," or a
demeanour,
"drunk and inc
or a "burglar
"manslaughter
ever he has to
the time. Esc
very rare, bec
it is almost im
to get away f
island, pursuit
ture are certair
an attempt to
the prisoner i
demned to w
rest of his term
heavy chain a
securely fasten(
legs. Inside
the prison reg
are most eas
and on our vis
we were strucl
absence of th
precautions to
escape. The

were low, and against them were placed lean-to sheds, tl
of which came to within six feet of the ground. All the
the cells were open—except those of a few persons await
for murder—and the prisoners were strolling about or l

into a passage in which was the entrance to the prison, whe
was stationed one solitary guard, armed with a short sword. V
found the two prisoners chatting together, looking out of t
window at the end of their corridor. One of the women pi
fessed to be a native "Kapoona," or witch-doctor; and h
murdered a man, a woman, and a young child with great bi

NATIVE DANCE.

tality and cruelty, gouging out their eyes with burnt sticks, a
partially roasting them, in full sight of a crowd of nativ
many of whom had assisted her. The natives firmly believ
her to be a "Kapoona," and did not, therefore, interfere w
her, because they considered she acted under some mysterio
influence. At one time it was thought that there would
difficulty in getting a jury of natives to convict her, and at h
trial she mentioned, as a proof of her claim to be a witch-doct
that rain, which was badly wanted at the time, had begun

told me, than New York or London, that the natives
understand or believe the Christian religion they profess.
they are well and strong they may appear to have given
old gods and idols; but when they are sick or in any
they turn to the gods of their fathers, just as did the I:
of old. The native witch-doctor is still an ins
and although through lack of the slightest knowledge of
or of medicine they oftener kill their patient than cure, t
not shatter the natives' faith. For such a disease as
fever a witch-doctor prescribes some such nonsensical i
as a black pig without a white spot, of a certain age, coo
certain way, and to be eaten by the patient at a certain
the day. After eating this the patient, needless to say, g
dies, and then the witch-doctor declare that this pati
two diseases—one the native disease which the pig
never fails to cure, and the other a " white man's "
which never fails to kill a native. Nor is this supersti
apparent fruitlessness of Christian teaching confined to 1
and ignorant of the natives. One would judge tha

native was a Chri:
heart, sincerely beli
the Christian religi
was free from the i
of native superstit
idolatry, it would be

Christianity as the late King, has gone in her own illn
with native witch-doctors and her suite to the volcano
Kilauea and to the crater of Halemoumou, "the abode
everlasting fire," where is supposed to dwell the nat
goddess Pele, whose aid she sought and to whom she turned
her extremity. This happened the very week before our visit
the volcano, and we learnt from eye witnesses the details of
pilgrimage. We heard that the Queen Dowager and su
reached Volcano House about four o'clock in the afterno

QUEEN EMMA'S BIRTHPLACE.

that they immediately started for Halemoumou, the Qu
being carried in a litter (her disease is partial paralysis), t
they arrived there at sunset, and took up their posit
on the edge of Halemoumou, immediately over-looking
burning lake, that the Queen was placed on the grou

goddess Pele. With a slight interval for food a
night, this was kept up until daybreak, when the whol
left. On other occasions parties of natives have gone th
have thrown into the burning lake, to the accompanir
chants and songs of the witch-doctors, pigs, fowls, and
of gin. Now, any belief in the efficacy of such appeals w
impossible if the natives thoroughly comprehended the C
religion they profess. The question arises, what are
learn from this? Are missionary efforts with native race
given up as entirely fruitless? Or is the above resu
what we might expect after seventy years of the stronge
sionary efforts that have been made in any part of the
It appears to me that this is exactly what we might expe
that therefore missionary efforts should not be given u|
must remember that nothing is harder to kill than super
and must not forget that even after a thousand years of C
teaching, we, in England, still believed in the power of v
and enacted laws for their punishment and death by b
At the same time, this would appear to point to the nece
giving at first greater attention to the material wants
people than to the inculcation of religious beliefs whic
mind has not the power to grasp and assimilate. It is a
choly fact that, notwithstanding all the efforts of the missi
the native population is decreasing at an alarmingly rap
It appears from the American Mission Report that in 18
had 900 schools in the Sandwich Islands and 50,000 s
This is exclusive of the English Mission schools. To-
total native population of these islands is barely 35,0c
women, and children. It is hardly possible to believe that
same amount of money, time, and labour been devoted to t
such of the arts and sciences of civilisation as would en;
natives themselves to make the most of their country,
raise themselves in the social scale, the native populatior
have sunk from 400,000 at the time of their discovery by (
Cook to 35,000 to-day. To hold the contrary opinion w
to admit that nothing can be done for the material well-b

religion, so that they may become a happy and prosper[ous] people, let us first teach them to make for themselves and fa[mi]lies the best use of their lands; let us make them into plant[ers,] cultivators, and manufacturers of such articles as can be m[ade] out of the raw material their lands produce; let us, in short, [act] as would wise guardians and trustees during the infancy [and] development of a ward. In this direction there is an enorm[ous] field for missionary effort.

The natives are passionately fond of music, and conseque[ntly] it is not surprising to find that the Government maintains a [very] fine band at Honolulu, which plays almost every night and on certain afternoons in some of the city squares and pa[rks.] Next to music, or perhaps it would be more correct to [say] equally with music, the natives love flowers. They m[ake] wreaths of them which they wear round their hats and ne[cks,] and on festive occasions men, women, and children are sir[ply]

natives for horses, and they are mos[t] horse riders. The ladies of all rank[s], the wealthiest to the poorest, ride stride like the men, and even E[nglish] ladies living in Honolulu get into th[e] fashion, and pronounce it to be mo[re com]fortable and easy than side-saddl[e.] [The] first time one sees a lady riding cros[s] it strikes one as very indelicate, b[ut] this first feeling has passed one is im[pressed] rather with the suitability of this [dress] in horse riding—there appears [great] freedom, and certainly the ladi[es are] thorough horse-women when gall[oping at] full speed. It is not unusual w[hen] driving to meet a tro[op of a] dozen or so of native [girls on] horse back, each cover[ed with] wreaths of flowers, s[inging] and laughing whilst th[ey gal]lop at top speed, e[vidently] thoroughly enjoying themselves. [They wear a] kind of divided skirt, very wide, [reaching] nearly to the ground when at [rest, but when] galloping it catches in the wind [and streams be]hind them -- increasing the [appearance of]  speed a[nd]

HABITS AND CUSTOMS.

COCOANUTS are a treat out here. Plucked green from
tree, the milk makes a capital drink and the nutty por
is quite soft and can be eaten with a spoon. The cocoa
flavour is not then so strong, but is much more delicate.
cultivated co
nuts, ca l
" educated "
distinguish t
from the " w
grow much sh
er, are not

are the greatest cultivators of them, as indeed they are o
all the vegetables raised here, with the exception pe:
oranges. On the outskirts of Honolulu, near Waikiki, t
a swampy piece of ground, which previous to the C
taking it in hand, was a dismal waste, growing notl
mosquitoes. The Chinese obtained a long lease of it, a
they have made it into one of the most fruitful and pr(
pieces of land on the Islands. The water was brackish
to its being on a level with and close to the sea, and a:
impossible to drain it, John Chinaman marked it out in(
nate ditches and banks, each about 15 feet wide, over tl
length of this land. Then he dug the sand and soil ou
space reserved to form the ditch, and piled it on t
reserved for the bank, sinking the ditch to a depth suffi
provide him with the soil required to raise the banks to ;
of 3 feet above the level of the water. I do not know tl
size of the swamp so treated, but should judge it to l
200 acres, from which some idea of the patient labou
Chinese may be formed. But when this preliminary w(
over, the work of reclamation had only begun. Rotatic
ping had to be gone through with the proper plants suit
drawing the salt out of the ground, and a free applic.
manure was needed to add the right constituents to the :
the same time John Chinaman has not forgotten to mak(
the water in the ditches, in which he rears large quan
fish—mullet, gold fish, and other suitable varieties, whils
surface of the water are reared thousands of young duck:
no doubt find the principal part of their food from the sh
insects on the banks and in the water. We can learn
many lessons from the Chinese, with whom nothing is
to go to waste. They make good tenants. In fact, one
man told me he would rather have a Chinaman for a tena
a white man, because with the former he was always sui
rent, and with the latter he was not.

Taro root is also largely cultivated by the Chinese, a
it is really a native product, and consequently one woul(

HABITS AND CUSTOMS.

cultivation are not plentiful, especially in some of the Islan
high rents for them are obtained. I heard of a rent of
dollars per acre per annum being paid by Chinamen fo
good plot. One crop only can be raised each year, and
the roots are gathered they are cut off from the stalks, wh

EATING POI.

are planted like cuttings in the ground, and make next yea
crop. The gathering and planting is all done under wat
generally about nine inches deep. After they are gathe
the roots are first boiled and then pounded by blows fr
a stone held in one hand, whilst between each blow
taro is moistened with water by the other hand. There d
not appear to be the slightest improvement anywhere on
Islands upon this laborious and primitive process which has b
handed down from generation to generation. This beating a
watering is continued for about two hours. At the end of t
time the taro is reduced to a sticky glutinous mass of a dirty g

before they eat it. This they do out of a large bowl or ca
each sitting round it cross-legged. Men, women, and c
dip their fingers into the same bowl, gathering up the poi
dexterous twist and conveying it to their mouths.
licking their fingers, the same process is repeated, and
until the meal is over. From this custom poi comes to b
according to its thickness and consistency, one finger p
finger poi, and three finger poi, the thick being eaten w
finger, the medium with two, and the thin with three
Some Europeans living out here eat it and acquire a lik
it, but the first taste is certainly not captivating. It st
the tongue and roof of the mouth and requires some e
gulp it down. The flavour is exactly like what one
expect to find to be the taste of bill-stickers' paste gor
It is, however, extremely nourishing and wholesome, a
natives are very fond of it. It has been their principal f
generations, and as they are a fine, well-nourished r
evidently possesses highly sustaining properties. I shou

clude that thei
of eating "pc
gether, by d
into one commo
accounts for the
of leprosy and
infectious disea
mongst the r
They are pe
indifferent to in
and will sit do
eat "poi" with
whose hands
that they are
advanced sta
leprosy.

It is interes
note how in th

The pigs become very like the wild boar, developing enorm[ous] tusks, and are often more than a match for the huntsman— fact, accidents at "pig-sticking" are rather numerous. T[he] dog in a few generations gets the slouching gait, moveme[nt] of the head from side to side, characteristic of the wolf. N[ot] only do the domestic animals run wild, but plants which in oth[er] countries are choice garden shrubs, here get the mastery [of] man and become a pest. Out of a single specimen of [a] lantana plant sent to a gentleman in Honolulu, and planted [in] his garden, this shrub has spread over all the islands so rapi[dly] that it has become a serious question how to get rid of it. [It] monopolises the ground wherever it goes, and entails great lo[ss] especially to the ranch men. Everything appears to run [to] extremes. Rats at one time were a plague, although they o[nly] got to the Islands within recent years from the trading shi[ps]. The mongoose was introduced to kill the rats, and having do[ne] so the mongoose now becomes as great a curse as ever the r[ats] were. The minah bird was introduced to kill the insects, a[nd] now the minah bird has increased to such an extent that i[t is] a greater scourge than the insects, and so on.

I suppose the Sandwich Islands must be one of the small[est] monarchies possessing a parliament and representative gove[rn]ment that the world can show. Imagine that country suppo[rt]ing a Queen, Royal Court, Parliament, Civil Service, and the modern machinery of executive government, with the us[ual] crowd of scheming office seekers and hungry place hunte[rs]. We cannot but smile at what appears a parody on mod[ern] institutions. Exclusive of the 37,000 Chinese, Japanese, a[nd] Portuguese plantation hands, who can hardly be called part [of] the nation, the total population, natives, half-castes, America[ns,] English, and Germans, only number 52,000. Every one of a[ny] standing out here is a "Right Honourable," or "His Excellenc[y]." The Queen holds receptions and distributes honours, orders, a[nd] badges, which no doubt are just as much use to the recipie[nt] as are our Orders of the Garter or the Thistle, and proba[bly] cause just as much jealousy and bitterness in those who do [not] receive them. There is a great deal of human nature in Roya[l]

not above "taking a drink" in a saloon with one of his s
provided the subject paid for it. Everything in the wo
question of size. If a thing is only big enough, we t
grand and dignified; if a thing is only little enough, we t
absurd and frivolous, and yet the only difference shall be
size. Hence we naturally smile at all this in the Sa
Islands, notwithsta
that we should be hig
dignant if foreigners
in the same way at our

Like San Fra
Honolulu possesses a
Town, but the China
of Honolulu is better
cleaner, and more s
than that of San Fra
The history of the C
here is an exact rep
of their history in the
First they are introdu
their cheap labour,
when their contract e
having acquired a
money by thrift and in
they enter into comp
with the white man a
chants, manufacturers
keepers, etc. Any vi
Chinese may have will
up with, except the
entering into comp
with the white mar
especially of beating

BANANAS.

his own field. This is an unpardonable offence, and imme
John Chinaman arrives at this stage of his history a
hurriedly pushed through the legislature prohibiting C

presented to us of labourers being objected to on the grou[nd]
that they are too frugal, careful, and industrious, and have
ambition and ability to raise themselves in the social scale

Japanese labour is now being tried, but I heard complai[nts]
to the effect that the Japanese will not be driven and forc[ed,]
that they rise against their overseers, and in some ca[ses]

JAPANESE COTTAGE.

have murdered them. The fact is, the Japanese, although v[ery]
little men, are game and full of spirit, and will not stand [the]
bullying system adopted on some plantations. Planters [say]
they are too touchy, want too much consideration, and
delicate handling, but I generally heard it admitted tha[t if]
they are properly and fairly dealt with, and not over dri[ven]
they make good workers.

Another class of plantation labour here is Portuguese. [These]
labourers were brought over under contract made by the gove[rn]ment, and the only complaint I heard against them was that t[hey]
were too dear, their contract rate of wages being about 18 t[o 20]
dollars a month, with two dollars extra for each child in t[he]
family after the first two. The planters complain very bitterl[y]

pay 30 dollars a month. One planter naïvely remarked that he did not object on principle to the Portuguese l large families, but that they over-did it. as they would have three children in two years.

The wages of the Chinese are about 15 dollars a mont those of the Japanese from 10 to 12 dollars a month. In ad all plantation hands receive house rent free. There are considerable number of natives engaged on the plantatior the fault with the native is exactly the lack of those qu which are objected to in the Chinaman. The native thrifty, he does not save or acquire wealth, and will no steadily and persistently from day to day. In view of facts it is not surprising that the planters, who do not f competition of the Chinese as merchants, manufacturer shopkeepers, and who only see in them the best pla hands they ever had. are now agitating to have the proh on Chinese immigration removed, asserting that if this done they cannot possibly carry on their plantations.

Sugar growing was commenced here practically, as l seventeen years ago, when the Reciprocity treaty wi United States was arranged. under which Sandwich sugar was admitted duty free into the States, the d sugar at that time bein cents a pound. Of this practically amoun

represents all other nationalities, natives included. The re[st]
is that the Islands are decidedly American in tone and sentim[ent]
and whilst the times are not yet ripe for annexation to the Sta[tes]
the tendency is all that way. For the last few years the Isla[nds]
have not had the benefit of the bounty, owing to sugar from o[ther]
countries being now admitted free into the States, and consequ[ent]
ly the planters are all complaining of "bad times," but it is har[d to]
see on what grounds, as the yield of sugar in the Sandwich Isla[nds]
is 50 per cent. over the average yield per acre elsewhere.

JAPANESE COTTAGE.

instance, a crop of ten tons per acre has been known there, a c[rop]
of five tons per acre is not uncommon, and a crop of three t[ons]
per acre is considered small; whilst elsewhere a crop of three t[ons]
would be considered high, and a crop of two tons is us[ual.]
What is really meant by " bad times," I suppose, is that it i[s no]
longer possible to have wasteful and extravagant managem[ent]
and dividends of 100, 200, or 300 per cent. per annum, as in [the]
old days of the bounty.

SANDWICH ISLANDS AND UNITED STAT

THE great question in the Sandwich Islands just n
can the United States Government be induced t
over Pearl Harbour, which is situated about 12 miles
Honolulu, as a naval coaling station. This project has
the appearance of being merely a gigantic piece of j
promoted by land speculators and others with land in

near Pearl Harbou
use an Americani:
thing is "being
for all it is worth.'
tentious plans of
City and Pearl H
are displayed at
public resorts.
plans show a fine ci
broad, handsome a
and streets with
sounding names,
railway station, pai
etc., all looking v
tractive on paper.
flowery words of t
spectus, "Pearl
the desired haven
artist and author
the invalid it is se
none, the perfect
which is so mu

Islands;" "Pearl City is the Paradise of the invalid;" "
Harbour, which the United States Government takes over
Naval Station." And then the promoters, coming dow
business, state that the capital is 5,000,000 dollars li
liability, that "the property offers an opportunity to s
holders to nett a handsome profit on a small amount of m
invested," and that it "gives positive security with as
increase in value." There then follows this remarkable
ment: "The United States Government will soon begin de
ing Pearl Harbour to admit of all kinds and sizes of ve

This harbour is to be the naval station of the Pacific fo
United States Government." And yet the States hav
even arranged for the harbour with the Hawaiian Govern
nor expressed any desire or intention of doing so.

We went by train to see this wonderful city, and
could not find it. Nothing daunted, we decided to try a

and the only inhabitant we saw was a Chinaman, who ⟨
ing as caretaker at the only house in the place. Tᵣ
streets and avenues were all marked out with stumps. ᴄ
boards, on which were lettered their pretentious names
the bushwood and scrub were still uncleared, and as these
were all more or less out of the perpendicular, they we
suggestive of tombstones over the dead hopes of the
holders than the origin of a fine city. Horses and
melancholy and very sad-looking, wandered listlessly
The only thing we found according to the prospectus ⟨
" perfect quiet," and if the invalid can " build up the syst
that he may find it a perfect paradise, but if he wants. in a
a roof to his head and a beefsteak or spring chicken tᴏ
must take train for Honolulu.

As to its attractions as a coaling station, no doubt it
suitable for that also when the harbour has been deepen
the bar cut through at a cost of a few millions of dollars
only the States can be "worked" to arrange for the wateᵣ
from the Hawaiian Government, there may be some pᴏꜱ
of this becoming an accomplished fact. Having done ᴛ
States will be able to arrange with the shareholders for
Pearl City, as it is clear they will want some land there.
the efforts of those disinterested men, who have pointed ᴏ
ideal coaling station to the United States Government,
rewarded, and the days of "assured increase in value" pr
in the prospectus will dawn for the shareholders. But
present it seems not unlikely that the whole thing will fᴀ
and consequently a great clamour is being raised in the
and elsewhere, in which the point discussed is app
whether it would be policy for the Hawaiian Governᴍ
make an arrangement with the States with respect tᴏ
Harbour, but in which it is clear that the real anxiety is
to attract the attention of the United States Governmeᴛ
that this anxiety is accompanied by a lively fear that theᵧ
succeed. It is impossible to say what the ultimate end
matter will be, but I can hardly imagine it possible tʜ

SANDWICH ISLANDS AND UNITED STATES.

America to Australia, New Zealand, China, Japan, and In
When the Nicaragua Canal is opened, their v:
will be still further increased, because they
cupy a central position on the new rc
that will then be available. But how(
events move with regard to the Sandv
Islands, it would be of undoubted advantag(
ourselves to make good our position with
gard to whatever points of vantage are
open for us. The circle is gradually narrow
first one power and then another gets a f
hold, and it certainly behoves us, who have

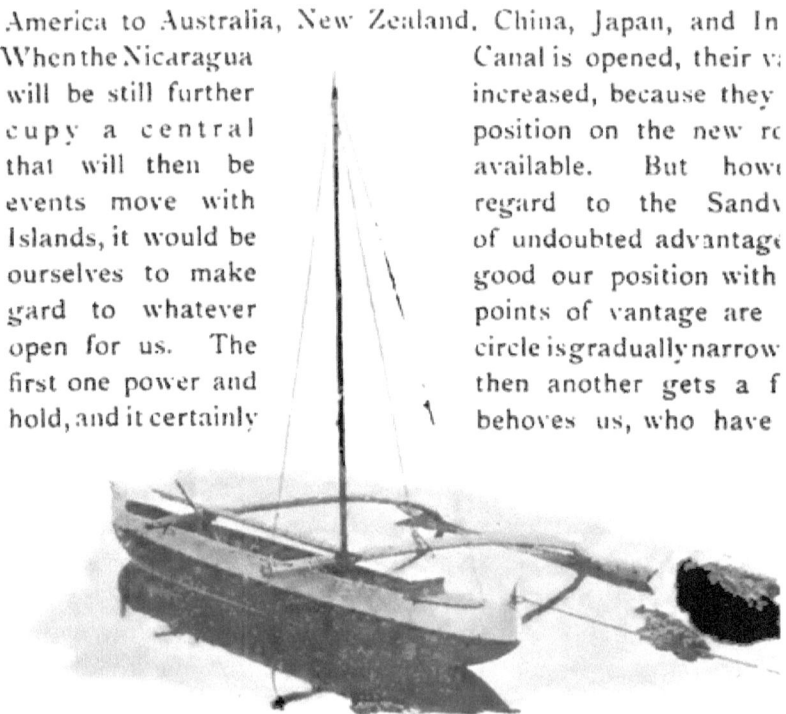

largest interests in the Pacific, not to let slip any opportunit
peaceably and quietly strengthening ourselves there.

VOLCANO OF KILAUEA.

WE had heard such glowing accounts of the grand majesty of the volcano of Kilauea, said to be the active volcano in the world, that we decided to see it for ou and took our berths in the little coasting steamer "G. W that goes every ten days to Punaluu, Island of Hawaii, the points from which the ascent to the volcano is mad description that was given us of the way the "Hall and rolled about in the channel was not encouragi fortunately either this had been exaggerated, or v favoured in the weather. The "Hall" left Hono

which we all heard so much at the time Sister Rose Gertru[de] went there. The lepers are well cared for, and are happy as as happiness is possible to people condemned to a living dea[th], for a leper once removed to Molokai is civilly dead. The w[ife] or husband left behind can marry again, and Governm[ent] divides the estate of the leper amongst the heirs just as if dea[th] had actually taken place. It is not surprising, therefore, t[hat] the natives try to avoid being taken, or have their friends tak[en] by every evasion in their power. This tendency is strengther[ed] by the fact that the natives hardly believe that leprosy [is] infectious. Married couples have been known to live toget[her] for years without communicating the contagion from one another, and I heard of one case where man and wife li[ved] together for 15 years, the one suffering from leprosy and fina[lly] dying of it, without communicating the disease to the oth[er]. Many people out here seem to think that leprosy is solely d[ue] to a low state of the blood brought about by living on coa[rse] food, salt fish, etc. But however difficult it may be to dec[ide] in which way leprosy is infectious, once taken by either wh[ite] man or native, there is no release for the victim until death en[ds] the unhappy life.

About six o'clock p.m., we arrived at the Island of Ma[ui] where some cargo was landed by the surf boats, and we p[ro]ceeded on our way. Close by is the Island of Lanai, in size abo[ut] 100,000 acres, used as a sheep run. This island was p[ur]chased by a delegate from the Mormon Church at Salt La[ke] City, who had been sent to the Sandwich Islands to found [a] Mormon settlement. It is reported that he was wise in [his] generation, and became possessed of considerable proper[ty] until at last the Church at Salt Lake got suspicious of him a[nd] sent out two of its members to inquire into matters and supersede him. On arrival they were well received by t[he] delegate who showed them the property. Finally they disclos[ed] to him their mission, and asked for an account of all the property [of] the Church, and called upon him to hand the deeds, etc., ov[er]. "Why certainly," was the reply they got, "and if you tell [me] what property the Church has got, it shall be done at once

The following day we arrived at the Island of Hawa[ii,] largest of the Sandwich Islands, and proceeded along the [coast,] landing and taking in cargo at the villages we passed. [We] stopped a little while at Kealakekua Bay, and most of us [went] on this historic spot, the scene of the first arrival and mur[der of] Captain Cook, and where a monument has been erected [to his]

CAPTAIN COOK'S MONUMENT.

memory. We ought to have arrived at Punaluu the same [day,] but there had been so many stoppages on the way that th[is was] impossible, and the ship anchored in a small bay from 8 [p.m. to] midnight, when we proceeded on our way, reaching Puna[luu at] 6 a.m. the next morning. The reason for this was that [at this] hour the sea calms down a little, the landing there at an[y other] being very difficult. We had to be landed in surf boats, a[nd the] trouble was to get into them. At one moment the sur[f]

don't get caught on the drop." However, we managed to
safely landed at last, and after breakfast at the little inn the
we proceeded to the railway station, the first six miles of
twenty-nine miles to the Volcano
House being done by rail. This
is a plantation line, and is the
most curious little railway
imaginable. The carriages
were open trucks, the third-
class passengers
having to sit on
their luggage and
hold on as best they
could, for there were
neither tops, sides,
nor ends to the car-

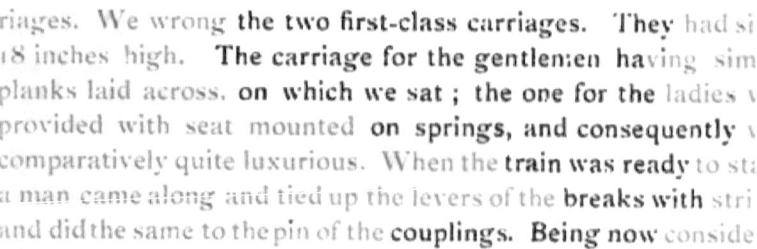

riages. We wrong the two first-class carriages. They had si
18 inches high. The carriage for the gentlemen having sim
planks laid across. on which we sat ; the one for the ladies
provided with seat mounted on springs, and consequently
comparatively quite luxurious. When the train was ready to st
a man came along and tied up the levers of the breaks with stri
and did the same to the pin of the couplings. Being now conside

ready, the train start
the engine puffing a
snorting, and sway
from side to side i
most rheumatical a
asthmatical mann
Where a gate blocl
our way the firen
jumped off the engi
ran ahead of the tr
and opened the ga
the train pass
through, he jumped
again, the guard at

We next took places in a coach something like a wag(
with a top to it, drawn by six horses, the driver being a
with an enormous whip, with which he could reach the lea
and which he cracked every few minutes, making a repor
a pistol shot. He was a tall, thin, bony Yankee, and as h
on the box with one leg hooked on the brake, the other h
against the footboard, one arm waving his whip above his

the other shaking the reins to urge on his horses, he l(
exactly like some huge human spider. The road was for a
all the way over lava beds, and was very rough and r
Some of the party had the wisdom to prefer going on horsel
those who didn't, and I was one of the latter, wished they
We never got such a bumping in our lives as on that ride
miles, which took us seven long, weary hours to accom
The road is so bad that in many places the driver
ferred to leave it and take his chance across the country,

quality of the road making. Most of us preferred to wa
rather than ride, and this we did the bulk of the way both goi
and coming. I thought if ever I met the man who made such
road, it would be some consolation to give him, in plain Lanc
shire, "a bit of my mind." But when I did meet him I fou
the road was punishment enough to him, and so I said nothir
He told me when he first came to this country there was
road of any sort, and he had to set to work to make one. Fi
he had to pay 1,000 dollars for right of way, then he had to p
the entire cost of making the road himself. He hoped to ma
a little from it by collecting toll, but he soon found that this w
impossible, and finally he abandoned all idea of doing so, a
now, except as a road to his own place—and others use
equally with himself—he does not get one cent. return from
He is now a wiser and a sadder man and has no doubt lear
the lesson that it is better not to do a thing at all than not to
it well.

VOLCANO OF HALEMOUMOU.

AFTER luncheon at Halfway Inn, we proceeded on our
arriving at Volcano House about four o'clock. We f
ourselves in very comfortable quarters and quite welcome
roaring wood fires prepared to greet us, for at this elev
(4,000 feet above the sea level) it was decidedly chilly. We
all too tired to do more that night than stroll about i

vicinity of the house, which we found to be built on a bl
the edge of the crater of Kilauea. The crater is four miles

LAVA FLOW.

to one end. We could see the smoke and the glare reflected the sky, and everything promised well for our visit the followir evening.

The country all around here is full of rifts and cracks, (
which issues sulphurous steam. Some of these blowholes
however, become dry, and some of the old ones are so g
over with ferns and brushwood as to make wandering

DRY VOLCANO RIFT.

from the beaten track a course only to be undertaken in day
Even then great caution is necessary. Horses and catt'
often lost, for the depth of these pitfalls is so great tha
impossible to recover them. On applying our hands to so
the smallest of the active blowholes, we found the heat
intense. We learned afterwards that all the hot water for the

a depth of four feet anywhere about here, steam issues throu[gh] the soil at once.

At 4 p.m. next day the party was formed, and accompani[ed] by two guides carrying lanterns, etc., we set off for Halemo[u]mou. First we descended the sides of the big crater for 5[00] feet, when we found ourselves on a level plain of lava, acro[ss] which we had to walk a distance of over two miles. T[he] formation of the lava here is much like that of an ice pack [of] some very large river. Here the lava was lifted up, there it w[as] sunk down. In some places slabs of lava were piled one on t[op] of the other. It had taken all sorts of curious shapes and form[s.] The colour also varied. In some places it was a dull, dirty gre[y,] in others it was a jet black, and shone like a polished stove; [in] others again the colour was a deep orange; and in others t[he] colour was that of burnt ashes. In some places the lava h[ad]

and rifts,
issued sulp
There the
hot, and di
over, ever
varying.
plodded in
route being
piles of brok

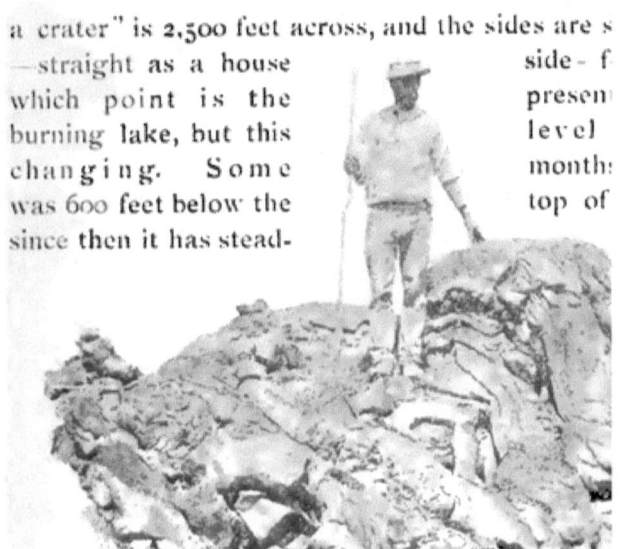

a crater" is 2,500 feet across, and the sides are s
—straight as a house   side - f
which point is the   presen
burning lake, but this   level
changing. Some   month:
was 600 feet below the   top of
since then it has stead-

rising, it is expected to be level with the top in a few month
The lake never overflows. Generally, when it is very hig
in the crater, an eruption breaks out in one of the mountain
on the Island, after which the lake falls again to its lowe

BURNING LAKE.

level. At the time we were there it was about 1,000 to 1,2
feet diameter, being surrounded by a beach—if I may be allow
to use the term—of 500 to 600 feet in width. It is quite i
possible to describe the scene. Around the shores of the la
the red molten lava was dashing like angry surf on a roc
bound coast, sending showers of molten spray some 20 to
feet high, and accompanying all this was the roar of the wave
rising and falling, now louder, now fainter, whilst the centre
the lake was alive with moving jets and fountains of molt
lava. Between these and the sides a thin crust of lava ke
forming as the surface of the lake cooled, to be broken up a

the sides of the volcano, and in the clouds of mist and s
that hung overhead, and also by the fact that the burning
was not only ever changing in appearance but also in ac
Sometimes for a considerable interval it would appear
quite dull, and the light and glow would almost fade awa
it was not long before it broke out again with renewed ac
It was a scene never to be forgotten. It was a veritable '
that burneth and fire that is not quenched."

After remaining two hours we set out to retrace our
homeward, each armed with a lantern, one guide leadin
way, the other guide following behind. It was now pitch
and however difficult the road had been in the daylight it v
nothing compared to the way back. However, on we
Indian file, the lanterns flickering, the leading guide ever
and then on reaching some blow hole raising the cry "
crack!" which cry was repeated in turn by each as the spo
passed. There is not the sli
danger, however. It is only a qu
of some little diffi- culty and exc
and we arrived safely at the
about 9.15. We were all read
supper, to which we did justice in
that proved that the solemnit
grandeur of the scene we ha
left had certainly not impaired

were scientific, some were flowery and gushing, some we poetical, and there was one description short, practical, and the point. It said simply "Rough on boots!" We looked our poor feet, and the truth of this was forced upon us. One our party had the sole of one boot completely worn off, and tl boots of all the others were in a far gone condition. The sha points of the lava cut into the leather like so many saws.

Next morning several of us set off to visit a forest of tr ferns about two miles from the hotel. We found it one tangl

FERN GULLY.

mass of ferns and creeping plants growing in tropical luxurianc Some of the tree ferns had stems 20 feet high, and the majorit were over 8 feet, the stems covered with numerous varieties c beautiful small ferns.

SAMOA.

THE following day we commenced the return jour[ney to] Honolulu, and left on Sunday, November 20, for Auc[kland.] We reached Samoa on Monday, Nov. 28, but had only

NATIVE BOATS (CATAMARANS) AT APIA, SAMOA.

hours there in which to go on shore. The natives at Sam[oa are] far behind in civilization those of the Sandwich Islands. [Great] numbers still live in the native grass huts, and dress in the

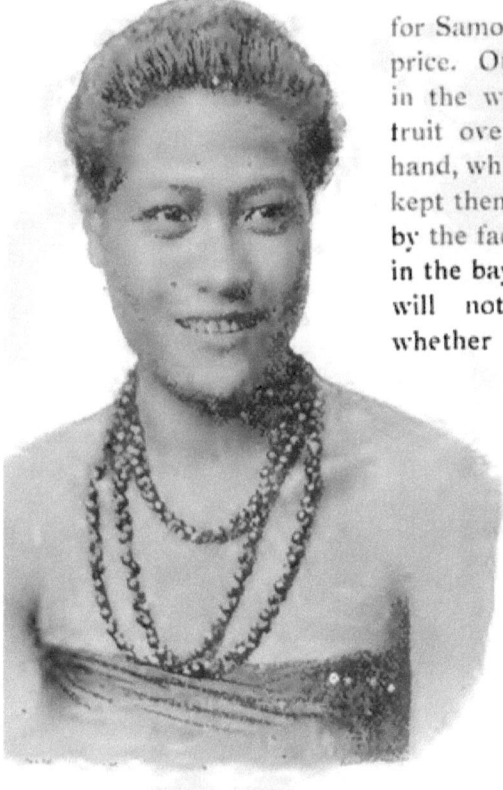

SAMOAN BELLE.

for Samoa, this was a prett price. Others of the natives in the water, holding bunc fruit over their heads wit hand, whilst with the othe kept themselves afloat, unde by the fact that sharks abc in the bay. It is said that will not touch a native whether the native is sh flavour or has too flavour I canno It is a fact that were there, b three were seer to the ship and 50 yards of whe natives were ming, and ne natives nor shark the slightest no each other.

The missic came *via* Aus degree they

who first landed at Samoa and on passing the 180th to have added a day to their calendar. This they omitted to do, and consequently were observing Sunday on Saturday. The setting right of this matter caused quite a struggle in Samoa, the missionaries offering the

under of having to explain their mistake to the natives, and having to tell them that the Sunday they had observed for yea was not a Sunday at all but a Saturday. This they feared wou destroy the native faith in Sunday altogether. However, t merchants insisted on the mistake being rectified, and, finall the missionaries giving way, this was done last year by holdi two fourth of July celebrations.

ARRIVAL IN NEW ZEALAND.

WE crossed the 180th degree in the night of Decemb[er]
and as we were travelling westward we had to dr[op the]
following day, Friday, December 2nd. So going to bed [on Thurs]day night, December 1st, on waking next morning we fo[und it]
Saturday, December 3rd.

We arrived at Auckland on Sunday afternoon, Decembe[r 4th,]
and were glad to have reached civilisation, letters, and teleg[rams.]
We found everything there to be more English—I had almo[st said]
than England—but certainly than any place we had seen [since]
leaving England. The hotel, the "Star," where we s[tayed]
is thoroughly English, and if we were not at home we [were]
certainly made as comfortable as we could be were we a[ctually]
there. The first person we saw on the quay waiting to we[lcome]
us was a friend we last saw in England four years before, [and as]
we had been entirely amongst strangers since leaving C[alifornia]
about the middle of October, this feeling of being at hom[e was]
increased by the happy meeting.

We are now at Wairakei, in the hot water distr[ict, the]
"Wonderland" of New Zealand. Just as at Kilauea all w[as fire]
and boiling lava, so here all is steam and boiling water, [with a]
smell of sulphur and hot flat irons. Close by is the h[ouse]
called the "Devil's Steam Hammer," where you hear a[nd feel]
the vibration of a constant "thud," "thud" beneath you[, just]
like some mighty force striving to break loose. I sup[pose it]
will go on "thud," "thud," until the ground gives away a[nd the]
whole lake is blown up. Another wonder, called the [""]
Geyser," is a pool of hissing, bubbling, boiling water that [every]
seven minutes spouts columns of water and clouds of [steam]
some 20 to 30 feet high. At another spot is the "

thousands of horse power—steam enough, in fact, to dr

needs no further description than the name; another name
"Twins" is so formed by a rock having fallen across the m
causing the jet of water to divide. Another is called
Champagne lake, because it is always bubbling like a
beaker of champagne. The waters are all colours, some
some green, others pink, while others combine two or
colours in various parts of the same lake. Others again
mud lakes bubbling and hissing, and oozing out a slatey cold
mud. All these lakes have strong curative powers that

known to the natives long before the advent of the white
The mud they eat as a cure for certain diseases, the waters
both drink and bathe in, and as the curative properties are

huge modern hotels, and has the advantage of being not o[nly] more homelike, but capable of almost any expansion. T[his] system, however, has one drawback—it can only be adopt[ed] where land is plentiful and cheap. We lived in a cosy lit[tle] cottage, built like the native "whare" or hut, the walls a[nd] roof of grass, the inside of reeds. The centre is the hall [or] dining room, out of which lead three bedrooms and a servi[ce] room. It is spotlessly clean, cool in summer, and warm [in] winter, and last, but not least, from the proprietor's point [of] view, very inexpensive to build. We had a little garden, which we saw in full bloom all the best of our old-fashion[ed] English garden flowers. It was hard to believe that we we[re] not in Devonshire or the Isle of Wight, but in the New Zeala[nd] mountains, so far removed from civilisation that even the ho[tel] horses had to be sent over 50 miles to be shod, and that, [as] a matter of fact, we were nearer to the Maoris than to t[he] white men. It is only ten years since this spot was sold [by] the Maoris to the late husband of the present proprietres[s,] Mrs. Graham, and since then everything has had to be broug[ht] here, roads made and trees planted, cottages built, and wh[at] was then a desert turned into a perfect garden. We all agre[ed] that it was the most comfortable place we could possibly desi[re.]

THE MAORIS AND THE LAND.

WE came to Wairakei from Auckland *via* Okoroire Rotorua. Auckland is a fine growing city immense possibilities for the future. We left Auckla[nd] Wednesday, December 7th, by train. The lines there narrow gauge railway of 3ft. 10in., and the carriages a[re] adaptation of the American plan, that is, one long saloon doors at each end. As we sped along there was wafted to [us] perfume of the new mown hay, sweet briars, and spring flo[wers] and we thought of December at home—wet and cold, or s[nowy] and sloppy—with something as near approaching a shiv[er] was possible on a warm summer day. On arrival at Oko[roire] our stopping place for the night, I took my first hot water followed by a dip in the cool river that flows past the bath h[ouse] and whilst I cannot say what the curative properties of particular spring may be, the combination of hot and cold tainly was a success as a "Pick-me-up" after nine ho[urs] travel.

The next morning we started early for Rotorua by the coach, and a magnificent drive it was through New Ze[aland] bush and over rolling plains. With the exception of settlements—one a sawmill, another the Halfway House one solitary farm, we saw no sign of man in all our six [hours] drive. Most of the land is exceedingly good, and the timb[er] the forests—red and white pine and other valuable woo[d] of immense size, some of the red pines being 15 to 20 f[eet] circumference at 6 feet above ground. All this is w[aste]

town population and home market, and then will come the time for the cultivation of the poorer lands. I say great care must be taken in the selection of land, because owing to its volcanic formation you find good land and poor land sometimes within a stonethrow of each other. On the way, we pulled up at a farmhouse and were regaled with baskets of beautiful fresh strawberries brought to the coach by a young lady probably the squatter's daughter—who offered them for sale with a grace at once so refined, delicate, and lady-like that, although we were out in the New Zealand bush, far removed from any sign of civilisation, it was the very embodiment of *la grande manière*. We arrived at Rotorua about 2-30, and after arranging for our rooms at the "Geyser Hotel," we at once proceeded to indulge in the luxury of hot baths. The hot springs here in the possession of the Maoris, who make a charge of 1s. each person, notwithstanding that the spot on which the bahouse is built is leased from them by the proprietor of t hotel, and at rather a stiff figure, as we were given to und stand. This looks suspiciously like charging twice over for t same thing. I may here remark that the Maoris are treat exceptionally well by the New Zealand Government in matters relating to their land, far better than any previo Governments in any other quarter of the globe have dealt w the native races. Every acre of land that does not belong the white man, by purchase or treaty, is viewed as belonging right to the natives. Now, whether the fact that the Mao were camping out on the land at the time that the white m came makes their claim to absolute ownership stronger th that of the white man, who, coming here, has, by his o exertions and industry, unaided in the slightest degree by t

land cannot be seized for any debts they may con
Not only do they not pay in the form of rates or other
anything towards the cost of road making, but are ac
paid for the land required to make the road, whilst
white man, when a road is made through his land, not
has to give the land required for that purpose, but als
pay in the form of rates and taxes the cost of ma
the road. This is carrying a just acknowledgment o
rights of landlords a little too far. It is not surprising ther
that we should see all the vices of landlordism develop
the natives, and that they should, as naturally as a
to water, take to that portion of our system of civili
which enables them to sit in idleness whilst their
are being developed and made of value without so
as their lifting their little finger, or even bearing any c
burdens of taxation that this development entails. He
New Zealand you find the native races occupying the su
position of landlords towards the white man, granting l
and drawing rents. Surely this is "unearned increment"
a vengeance, for the land had practically no value till the
man came. I heard of one native who was said to be dra
£5,000 a year in rents. I heard of another who refus
renew a lease, after the tenant had spent large
on the property, except at a greatly increased rental. I hea
other natives who still own building land in Wellingtor
other large cities, and who have risen to the opport
afforded them and refused to sell, knowing that every day
property increases in value. Undoubtedly much could be
in support of the Maoris' claims to ownership, and it wou
out of place for me to go further into the question th
record how the matter stands, so far as I have been ab
gather information, and, of course, subject to correction s
I have been misinformed as to the exact details.

Having paid our 1s. 6d. each and entered our nam
the book, we took our bath, and afterwards strolled q
through the Maori village. Here the natives do their co

until it is sufficiently cooked, when they carry it home and ea
it. I did not see a single fire in the whole village. Ho
housewives at home must envy the sweet simplicity of thi
domestic arrangement! No smell of cooking in the house, n
getting up at five o'clock to light the fires, the water always o
the boil day and night, week-day and Sunday, and all tha
is necessary being merely to pop the things to be cooked into

COOKING.

bag, suspend it in the water, go and have a smoke or a gossip
and come back to find the dinner ready for eating. There is, o
course, the trifling disadvantage that sometimes the childre
tumble into these holes, even whilst playing in their own littl
garden, and are seen no more. But this is only a detail whic
may or may not be a disadvantage, according to the views th
parents hold with regard to what are often, even in Englanc
described as "encumbrances." Here and there we saw poo!
—not hot wells—but merely holes, in which overflow water fro!

necessity of providing themselves with the luxury of dre
rooms. There is nothing the native delights in so much
hot bath, and it is wonderful how correct they are in
knowledge of the properties of the different hot springs.
instance, the bath called at the Sanatorium, "Madame R

BATHING.

because of its beautifying effect on the skin, has been kno
the natives for generations by a name which, literally tran
is "Young Maiden's Skin," signifying that it makes th
soft as that of a young girl. In the village we met a ta
old savage known as the "Bone Scraper." After a
dies the body is buried for two years, when it is dug u
the flesh scraped off the bones, which are then deposit
the top of certain high mountains, the exact spot being
only to the particular tribe to which it belonged. The

like pig, "only nicer." He seems to have been a bit of a epicure in his way, because he complained that "white ma tastes salt," but he added, "Maori never." Probably he happene to fall on a party of early settlers who had been living on sa pork during the six months voyage out. His face wa beautifully tatooed, and it certainly did not at all detract fror his appearance, but rather the contrary. The practice of tattoo ing appears to be fast dying out, and we did not see any o the young men ornamented in this way.

"BONE SCRAPER."

WAIOTAPU.

THE next day we drove to Waiotapu, a long drive c twenty miles, but it is such a wonderful region that w more than repaid for the visit. The whole country to be one huge deposit of sulphur, silica, alum, and othe stances. One mountain seems to comprise the whole glows in the sun a mass of gorgeous colouring, which gi it the name "Rainbow Mountain." The geysers are nur and wonderful, and here we saw two that spouted miner The most wonderful fact is that these geysers—some some sulphur, some alum, silica, etc.—are often side b and yet are quite distinct in their properties and characte Here we saw in miniature some pink and white terraces give one a very fair idea of what must have been the ef the celebrated ones that were destroyed in 1886. terraces are formed by the overflows from the geysers, wl process of hundreds or thousands of years deposit a harc ing of the substance with which the water is impreg Some of the lakes here are a deep blue colour, others pink, milk white, or black. After we had visited all the our Maori guide struck a match and held it to a blow-ho of which was issuing very little vapour. Immediately followed a great rush of steam. This was repeated ove over again, with various blow-holes, and always wi same result. I tried to get some explanation of this nomenon, but no one here seemed to be able to exp satisfactorily. The Maori, however, had his explanatic when I asked him why it was so, he at once said, witho

on a crust of very uncertain thickness in some places hundreds of feet thick, in others only a few inches. Occasionally accidents happen, and a foot breaking through the crust as through thin ice, slips into the boiling water that bubbles beneath, and gets badly scalded. One of our party slipped in this way, but fortunately he recovered himself quickly, and happily without damage. This had the effect of making us all extremely cautious to follow in the exact footsteps of the guide during the remainder of our stay there.

ERUPTION OF TARAWERA.

WE had heard ever since arriving in this Hot Water W
land such accounts of the departed glories of the Pi
White Terraces, destroyed in one night by the eruption of
Tarawera, June 10th, 1886, after having probably exist
thousands of years, that we decided to make an excursior
and see the handiwork of volcano and earthquake on a
scale. Formerly, tourists travelled by coach over a good
But now the road exists no longer. In some places it is swa
up in a yawning abyss. In other places it is cut right in t
a crack 30 to 60 feet wide that follows the centre of the ro
miles. So there was nothing for it but to go on horseba
give up all idea of making the journey. But none of the
could lay the slightest claim to being able to ride a
Some never had ridden in their lives. Others remen
having ridden ponies in their youth, and having still a
recollection of the tricks the ponies resorted to in order
rid of them, hardly felt equal to renewing their part in th
formance. One of the party declared that whenever he v
horseback he was always, like the sailor, paying out or h
in the slack of the reins. He said if the horse lifted up its
he seemed to have reins long enough for half-a-dozen l
and didn't know what to do with the surplus, but that
horse stopped to eat a little clover by the roadside (and h
the horses he had given him to ride always did take that li
then the reins grew so plaguey short that he was nearly
over the horse's head. When he pulled hard to convince
it was about time to move on, his horse would turn its

However, our guide promised to give each of us the sure
footed little Maori horses that are able to find the road just a
well without a rider as with one, and so we all felt bold enoug
to decide to go. And, I may here say, as showing how well th
horses did their work, that the first words uttered by a grey
haired venerable gentleman on our return were that his onl
regret was that he could not give his horse five shilling
because, h
said, "
deserve
it." As
proof of th
he mentio
ed that
one poir
of the ro
home, •h
being tl
last of the
party got on
the wrong
path, and
that, after
proceeding
along it for
about 200
yards, his
horse stop-
ped, shook

PINK AND WHITE TERRACES.

its head, and without even so much as waiting to ask his lea\
turned quietly round and retraced its steps until it struck t

sweet briars mingled with them in a way that made it diff
believe we were not in some Devonshire or Cheshire lane
air was beautifully fresh, but the sky was cloudy, and we
occasional shower in the morning, but the afternoon an(
ing were bright and clear. We soon reached the (
affected by the eruption; here and there the trees and
were buried beneath the storm of ashes and pumice du
rained down from Mount Tarawera that awful night. T!

WHITE TERRACES.

itself had split right down the centre, so that it is now n(
but a yawning chasm. This rift follows the centre of th
for fully three miles, and at first it appeared to me th
cleavage had followed the break in the earth's crust cau
making the road, just in the same way that the cleavag
stone will follow the groove made by the mason's chisel,
little closer examination showed me that the rift follow(
road only for so long as the road was in the centre of the

spot where it looked impossible for man or horse, or indeed for any living creature other than a chamois, to get past. It was a a place where a huge crack went deep into the sides of a mountain in the form of a wedge or letter V. Along the sides of this a narrow path, not more than two feet wide, had been notched out, but constant use and rain storms had worn this path almost away. To reach the first arm of this V-shaped crack there was a very sharp descent—so sharp indeed that it was quite a scramble down—followed by the quick turn of the corner almost at right angles on to the narrow ledge running round the sides of the cleft in the mountain. In going round the corner one of the horses got too much speed on, and in turning actually got one leg over the precipice before being able to pull himself together. The rider had hardly time to shout out " I'm going over," when the horse recovered himself and proceeded quietly and cautiously along the narrow path, and reached the other side in safety. I suppose there was not the slightest danger. The guide said there never had been an accident, and argued therefrom that such a thing was impossible, and he ought to know. Certainly, the horses knew the way perfectly, and were so sure-footed that they might be trusted to take themselves and riders safely over paths where it would positively be dangerous for the riders to walk on foot. Notwithstanding this we all breathed more freely when we got safely past the place on our return journey, and one of the party was heard to declare that no money should tempt him over there again.

We reached Wairoa in good time, but what a scene of desolation it was. Formerly this was the busiest tourist headquarters in New Zealand, for all the world went to see the Pink and White Terraces, not to have seen which, for anyone with the slightest claim to being a "globe trotter," was equivalent to not having seen Niagara, or London, or Paris. Here there were on the night of June 9th, 1886, two hotels, a church, and a happy prosperous village. But on the following morning all was buried, with little remaining to mark the spot. Those who saw the terraces in all their glory say that there is nothing now left in the whole of this district worth the journey

though the road was, than ever before. We pictured t[he] selves the scene of the evening of June 9th, 1886, ever [so] peaceful and quiet ; the hotels with their usual complem[ent of] tourists eager for the morrow and their visit to the famo[us] races ; the natives in their "whares" calculating how [much] their work as guides and boatmen would be worth to the[m;] the centre of all stood the little village church, the villa[ge] with its water wheel giving a suggestion of civilisation, c[omfort] and prosperity to the scene. It was exactly the same [in] appearance as on any other ordinary night, and no one dr[eamt] of danger, much less was prepared for it. We heard fr[om an] eye witness that about one o'clock in the morning of June [10th] everyone was aroused by Mount Tarawera being in eruption. Hastily dressing, tourists from the hotels and [natives] from their "whares" flocked to a point of vantage the be[tter to] view the grand and awe-inspiring spectacle, little thinkin[g that] it could possibly affect themselves, who were a good [many] miles away, and with Lake Tarawera between them a[nd the] burning mountain. But soon the air was filled with clo[uds of] falling pumice, sand, and cinders, and the ground was h[eaving] convulsively under shocks of earthquake. In the panic [that] ensued no one knew where to go or where to hide, for the[re was] no place that appeared likely to be more secure than ar[iother.]

feebleness and impotence as great as that of the very lowest c God's creatures. The shocks of earth-quake grew worse, the showers of dust and ashes heavier, and all except Mr. Bainbridge left the hotel and fled to a native "whare." fearing each moment that the hotel, although built of wood, stout and firm, would collapse and bury

WAIROA HOTEL, AFTER EXPLOSION.

them. After this Mr. Bainbridge appears to have commenced t write a letter. which was found next day unfinished. when a quive of greater force than any before shook the hotel to its foundatior He rushed out and was caught and buried beneath the fallin verandah. He was the only European killed; all the re: escaped, even without a scratch, in the native "whares" c huts. which equally well withstood the earthquake and th falling ashes.

We found the place in exactly the same state it has been i ever since that awful night. The once prosperous village lie buried beneath the volcano ashes. There we saw just the to of the village mill and the water wheel, but the stream th: drove it has disappeared, and only the top rail of the little bridg that crossed the rushing waters can be seen. The nativ "whares"—all but one that stands solitary and desolate on rising piece of ground—are completely entombed beneath th showers of sand and cinders. The hotel is buried almost to th bedroom windows. The ashes appear to have drifted like sno before a gale, so that here and there you may see garden gate showing above the ground, but not a vestige of a hut or house

dug out—who can tell—some hundreds or thousands of
hence, like a second Pompeii. In some places the ashe
sand thrown out by the volcano have covered the land 2c
deep; in others they lie only like thin dust on the ground.
whole country round has the appearance of being envelopec

THE OLD MILL.

dirty snow—snow, that is, such as falls near a smoky city.
a native or white man is now to be found through a
region; everywhere is desolation and barrenness, and it
take centuries before any depth of soil can accumulat
clothe the surface. First we noticed come the ferns grow
crevasses here and there, then other plants, and so on
nature shall have covered with fertile soil this bare and de
region, making it again ready for the use of man.

We decided to cross the lake and explore Mount Tara
Unfortunately, after making the eight miles in the bc
began to rain, and the highest point of the mountain v
enveloped in mist that we were compelled to abandon all i

it is to-day. The fire is still there, and on poking a stick in
the sides of the mountain and drawing it out again, the end w
found to be burnt and charred. The whole place looks "u
canny," and we were all glad—although, no doubt, we should n
have confes
ed so mu(
to each oth
— when v
began to r
trace o(
steps dov
the side
the mounta

CARVED HOUSE.

VILLAGE SCENE.

We rowed
again across
the lake, and
we climbed up
to Wairoa, but
on our arrival
there we found
that several of
the horses had
broken loose and rambled off, which was certainly another pro
of their intelligence, for as far as grass or vegetation w.
concerned, they might easily find a better place. However, th(
were captured at last by the Maoris, and we finally all arriv(
at the hotel in safety, after what, to our town and city muscle

NAPIER TO DUNEDIN.

AFTER leaving the Hot Lake district at Wairakei we t[ook] by coach to Napier, through some of the finest imaginable, over mountain tops, along roads that ov[er] deep precipices and valleys, down magnificent gorges and skirting New Zealand bush, profuse in wild flowers a[nd] ferns. Seated beside the driver, viewing all this, the coach rattling along at a speed that makes everyone except the driver feel nervous, re-

pieces of road-making are to be met with, but probably a stretc[h] of five miles in length, reached about two hours before enterin[g] Napier, is the most remarkable road the world can show. In th[e] short length we had to ford—there are no bridges—the river E[s] and one of its tributaries no fewer than forty-six times. Th[e] road traverses a deep valley, through which the river winds an[d] twists, first touching one side of the valley then the other, side[s] so precipitous that it was impossible to make a road on eith[er] one or the other, except at an enormous expense. Cons[e]quently the way is made down the centre of the valle[y] crossing and re-crossing the river in a seemingly endle[ss] succession of fords—no light work for the horses nor ea[sy] task for the driver. At each crossing there is first t[he] sharp run down the bank, then the plunge into the river, full [of] treacherous holes, which varying in position after each floo[d] the driver is expected to know and avoid with the skill of [a] pilot. In ordinary times the water flows freely over the axl[es] of the wheels, but in flood times the water rises much highe[r] and then the passage can only be made heading down strear[m] otherwise, as the water flows through the coach, the hors[es] could not make way against the stream. A new road is no[w] being constructed by the Government along a route whi[ch] avoids this river altogether. We felt fortunate in travellin[g] before it was finished. Good roads are not nowadays a novelt[y] even in the colonies. A road such as we had just passed ov[er] we may never meet with again.

We found Napier to be built on land jutting out into a ba[y] so that there is a harbour on one side of the town, and a fi[ne] sea beach on the other, reminding us on the sea side very mu[ch] of Llandudno, only that the hill representing the Great Orm[e] Head is nothing like so large. Our next journey was [to] Wellington, thence we crossed to the middle or South Islan[d] and on to Christchurch, which is such a thoroughly South [of] England Cathedral town that one can hardly believe it to be [in] New Zealand and not in England. From Christchurch [to] Dunedin—a second Edinburgh, only lacking, of course, t[he] fine view from the Princes Street of the modern Athens. N[o]

NAPIER TO DUNEDIN.

were decorated with evergreens in true Christmas fashion, t streets were crowded with eager purchasers of Christmas car(and of toys to be given in the name of Santa Claus, but to vi(all this with the sun shining bright and strong until long after eight o'clock at night, the people in print dresses, muslins, and summer sui with nothi to sugge Father Chri mas, cover with frost a snow, made all look lik(hollow sha a mere m querade Christmas

AT CHRISTCHURCH.

and a very poor one at that. We felt inclined to take some the rising generation aside and ask them if they knew wl Christmas really ought to be like.

From Dunedin we went to the Lake Wakatipu, in district called the Switzerland of New Zealand, and after a sh stay far too short to become fully acquainted with the beaut

NEW ZEALAND'S LABOUR GOVERNME[NT]

THERE is a story told of a Frenchman saying to his [English] host, "If I were not a Frenchman, I should wish t[o be an] Englishman," and of his host replying, "If I were [not an] Englishman, I should wish to be an Englishman." Th[at which] we see of New Zealand, its climate and people, the m[ore we] feel constrained to say that if our home was not in Engla[nd we]

should wish it to be in New Zealand, and we also feel that those who have their homes there might with trut[h]

beauties and wonders we have nothing even to compare w
what is to be seen in New Zealand. We agree with the prophe
that in the future it will be the Britain of the Pacific.

New Zealand is a very paradise for the working man—in t
sense that the working man is the man who will work. The
is no place there—as Mr. Gladstone recently stated there w
not anywhere in the whole wide world—for the idle wealt
man, known in New Zealand as the "Social Pest." Rece
legislation has been specially directed to prevent the pos
bility of his gaining a foothold in the country, throu
acquisition of the broad acres of New Zealand.

The Government there is essentially a working ma
government—from the Premier downwards. The majority a
themselves working men. Some are compositors, some boi
makers, one is a lamp lighter, one a packer in a store, and so on.
is said of one that he was actually at work inside a boiler, drivi
home the rivets, when the paper announcing his appointme
was handed to him. And yet I must say, for the benefit
those who would expect the contrary, that I found it to
generally admitted that it is one of the best governments N
Zealand has ever had. There have been no revolutiona
measures—unless, indeed, the graduated land tax be so call
—the country is more prosperous than ever, and as far as I c
gather, the electors are likely to renew their confidence in t
Government at the next election. Undoubtedly, as might
expected from a government representing the democrac
differences have been made in the incidence of taxation, where
incomes and property below certain values are either entir
relieved from taxation or have to pay only on a reduced sca
whilst large incomes and large estates pay on a higher a
gradually rising scale. But this must appeal to all of us
merely just and right, and not an abuse of power such as
at home have suffered under, when, the power being in t
hands of the wealthy landowners, the incidence of taxati
was so arranged that the greater burdens should fall on t
backs of the people, whilst the wealthy landlords shou
escape almost entirely free. Of course there are many people

tax, whilst those with small incomes pay either sixpence
pound or nothing, according to the degree of smallness o
incomes!! I cannot but think that their dismal foreb
spring mainly from the fact that their own pockets are to
As to such a tax driving capital out of the country, the
too absurd. So long as New Zealand can offer a goo
and a fair return to capitalists they will not leave.

GRADUATED LAND TAX.

BUT there is another tax directed to reach the wealthy, bu which altogether differs in principle from the income tax, ar that is the graduated land tax. New Zealand suffers, althoug not to the same extent as do the Australian Colonies, from the fact that there are there a number of very large estates held by private individuals and by wealthy companies. The tendency of this is to keep out small squatters. The owners, say, of estates of 50,000 acres and upwards, will not divide their estates, knowing that the value of their property is increasing by leaps and bounds owing to the rapid development of the country. Undoubtedly to hold

increased value of their land. But the fact is in many ca:
rather retard than promote the progress of the country.
the nation as a whole has to be active and energetic, some c
who hold these large estates, on the contrary, feel that th
policy is a waiting one — that time, in fact, will do more fc
than they can do for themselves. All this tells against
vancement of the country, and the present Governmen
had to seek for a solution of the difficulty. Not eve
strongest supporters would hold that the graduated lanc
a perfect measure. Still it appears to be likely, judgin
results already obtained, to realize the object in view—r
the ultimate splitting up of large estates into a number o
ones. We must not forget that it was the Governmen
selves that sold the land to the owners of these large
Therefore, although they have now discovered their err(
passed a law which, in the future, limits the sale of Gove
land to not exceeding 2,000 acres to any one person, it i
that they must act fairly and honourably by those to who
willingly sold large tracts of land in the early days of the
The Conservatives claim that the Labour Party, by pass
graduated land tax, have broken faith with the owners o
estates, and they make their opposition to this tax one
strong points of their case against the Government.

 I will endeavour to explain the tax and its bearings, b
it appears to me to be one of the most important measures
ing the future of New Zealand, either for good or ev
could possibly be devised. I find from the Official Handl
New Zealand, 1892, that first there is a "Land tax of one
in the pound on the actual value of land, a deduction
allowed to each owner of the present value of improvem(
to £3,000, and an owner is also allowed to deduct any a
owing by him, and which is secured by a registered mo
In addition to the above deductions, there is an exemp
£500 allowed when the balance, after making deducti
stated, does not exceed £1,500; and above that a small
tion is allowed, but it ceases when the balance amo

graduated land tax commences with a tax of one-eighth of penny in the pound when the value is £5,000 and under £10,000, and rises on a graduated scale, increasing by one eighth of a penny in pound for every £10,000 to £20,000 increase in value. When the value reaches £210,000 the tax is one penny-three-farthings in the pound. Beyond this there is no further increase in taxation. From this it will be seen at once how heavily this tax presses on large estates, and how very lightly on small or moderate sized ones, which is in fact the very object the Government have in view. Thus, for instance, a estate of the value of say £8,000 would pay one penny in the pound property tax and one-eighth of a penny in the pound graduated tax, amounting together to £37 10s. 0d.; but a estate of the value of say £240,000 would have to pay one penny in the pound property tax and one penny-three-farthings in the pound graduated land tax, amounting together to £2,750, that is to say, it must pay over seventy times the amount in taxes although only thirty times the value. And supposing such a estate in New Zealand could be looked upon as a five per cent investment, the owner would have to pay close on 5s. in the pound out of his income to the Government. But if he was not so fortunate as to own his own estate clear of mortgages his position becomes quite untenable, for he cannot deduct anything on account of any mortgage from the amount of the graduated tax. Thus, if his estate were mortgaged for three-quarters its value, say £180,000, after deducting this from the amount due on property tax he would find, supposing he paid 5 per cent interest for the mortgage, that out of his nett income of £3,000 he must pay £2,000 in taxes, that is, 13s. 4d. in the pound Should he value the estate at less than the Government he can force the Government to either buy his estate at his own valuation, or reduce their valuation to the same amount. This portion of the Act has already been taken advantage of by some owners of large estates, and during our stay in New Zealand most notably by the Trustees of the Cheviott Estate. This estate of over 80,000 acres, was valued by the Government £300,000, and by the owners at £260,000. The Government

excellent land, well suited for cutting up into small farms
of course it will be of much more value to the country, a
employment and food for thousands more people than
present state as a sheep farm, employing only a compa
small number of hands as shepherds, shearers, etc. No
this sale appear a particularly hard one for the vendors,
am informed, gave originally some ten shillings an acre
land (say £40,000), which with £45,000, the assessed v
improvements, leaves the good sum of £175,000 profit t
credit, for what may fairly be called "unearned increment
cases would not probably show so favourably for the ven
this one. It certainly appears to me that to prevent in
being done some extension of the power to force the C
ment to purchase at a fair valuation should be grant
owners of estates affected by the graduated land tax
Government have discovered their error in selling large
ties of land to single individuals, but the large estates
created by purchase from themselves or the Maoris, and
case acknowledged by themselves, it would appear that t
course open to them was to offer now to the owners the
of either selling back at the present fair value, or payi
graduated tax. I do not know and could not get infor
as to how the man stands who rents say 100,000 (as m
from the Government, nor what amount he has to pay in
but it is quite clear that when leases for such land fall
Government will be free to deal with them as they consid
for the public good. The object of the graduated la
being the "greatest good of the greatest number," a
settlement of the country with a number of small farmers i
of a few large ones, undoubtedly the Government cannot
to deal other than fairly by those who bought these large
from them in perfect good faith, and I have no doub
should the graduated land tax be found to press une
such inequality will be remedied. But there is one q
that may perhaps be asked in considering this matter, an
is, why there should not be a corresponding tax on other
of property? As far as I can gather, £10,000 investe

GRADUATED LAND TAX.

varies the incidence of taxation as between one class of [p]
and another. Therefore, to correctly understand the gr[
]land tax, we must consider it not as a tax, but as a [
]framed to discourage the holding of large landed estate[s
]viewed from this standpoint, and as an absolute necessity [
]proper development and settling of the country, it appears [a
]good and useful act, and one that certainly tells no more [
]against the interests of large landowners than did the r[
]the Corn Laws with regard to the same class in Englan[d
]necessity in each case was the same,—the progress and a[
]ment of the nation, and the well-being of the masses, [
]attaining these ends any immediate and temporary loss [
]classes might suffer was not for one moment allowed to [
]the way of reform. That really there is not any ver[y
]inequality in the New Zealand system of taxation, apart f[
]penalty entailed on the holding of large estates, can [
]best be illustrated by taking for comparison one of our lar[
]wealthiest commercial undertakings — say Guinness's [
]and the land of one of our wealthiest proprietors—say [
]known Duke. It is impossible to give the exact value [
]two properties, but this will not in any way affect the cor[
]of the illustrative comparison. We will therefore supp[
]the present market value of Guinness's brewery, as rep[
]by the quotations of the shares, is between £13,000,[
]£14,000,000, and the nett annual income £750,0[
]will also suppose that the present value of the [
]landed property is between £13,000,000 and £14,000,0[
]which the nett annual income would probably not [
]£400,000. If these two properties were in New [
]Guinness's brewery would pay in direct Imperi[a
]£37,500 a year, or five per cent. on the nett inco[
]the Duke's property would pay in direct Imperi[a
]£150,000 a year, or 37½ per cent. on the nett [
]But if the Duke came to the conclusion, as he [
]would, that this tax made large landed estates into a [
]investment, he would sell out. Supposing the estate wa[s
]

would probably invest the proceeds in **Government, railway, a****other** securities, yielding him **his original nett** income £400,000 a year, on which he would then pay only £20,000 year in direct Imperial **taxes**, instead of £150,000. **This res**clearly shows that **the intention of** the graduated land tax to make the holding **of** large **landed** estates practical impossible. **At the same time the holding of** landed estates moderate **size is not impossible—the tax on an estate of s**£48,000 value, would **be** £325 **a year—a heavy** tax certain **but not entirely** prohibitive.

The principle embodied **in the** graduated land **tax is t key note to a great** deal **of** the legislation **of the Labour Par in New Zealand. But,** unfortunately, through some **of the ac they have passed with a similar** object the proverbial **coach a****six can be driven.** For instance, there is an act called "**one m****one run**" (*i.e.*, one farm), which provides that **no man sh****purchase** or lease **from the Government** more than 2,000 **acres good** land, or such a quantity of poor land as would carry 5,0 sheep. This act **gives splendid** scope **for** what is known "dummying,"—that is, purchasing as **many** 2,000 acre or plots as the purchaser wishes to hold **in** the names of frien and relatives, **acting as** "dummies." **If, however, a** case "**dummying**" **can be** proved, those **convicted can be sever****dealt with by the law,** but then unfortunately **it is not ea to prove** "dummying," **especially if the** "**dummies**" a **relatives. Another** act, the spirit **of which** is often broken, **one which provides** that where two **or more persons apply f the same plot of land,** the plot shall be balloted **for. Former** this difficulty **was settled** by selling the plot to the man w **would** give **the highest** price for it, but **it was** considered th **under** this system none except **men** of means had the slight **chance.** Therefore, with **the** intention **of** giving an equ chance to rich **and poor alike,** a law was passed providi **that such lots be balloted for,** each applicant depositing 10 p **cent. of the value at the time of** making his application. Capi **was not long in seeing a loop-hole here, and of** taking advanta

old.' He has, however, the consolation of knowing t
often the "biter gets bitten," as when one of the "d
proving an exception to the rule which states that '
always honour amongst thieves." refuses to hand over
he has won to the "dummier," who under such circu
can only "grin and abide." He has, of course, no
against the "dummy."

MAORI SALUTATION.

LABOUR LEGISLATION.

THE Government, amongst other measures, has founded [a] Labour Bureau, and no doubt there will be plenty of usefu[l] work for such a department. In England we have Boards [of] Trade, Boards of Agriculture, Foreign Office, Colonial Office[,] and scores of other departments; and yet, although labour i[n] one form or another is the lot of ninety-nine out of ever[y] hundred able-bodied adults in the kingdom, we had n[o] until recently any Government department specially const[i]tuted to deal with labour questions. From a speech of on[e] of the members of the New Zealand Government, I no[te] the special duty of the bureau to be as follows:—"A[re] there trees in one part of the Island to be felled or lan[d] 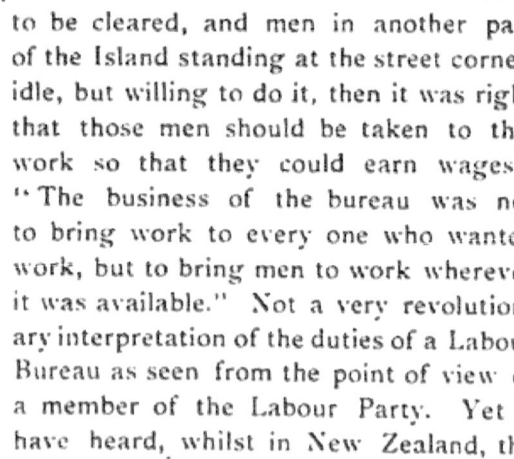 to be cleared, and men in another pa[rt] of the Island standing at the street corne[r] idle, but willing to do it, then it was rig[ht] that those men should be taken to th[e] work so that they could earn wages[.] "The business of the bureau was n[ot] to bring work to every one who wante[d] work, but to bring men to work wherev[er] it was available." Not a very revolution[-] ary interpretation of the duties of a Labo[ur] Bureau as seen from the point of view [of] a member of the Labour Party. Yet [I] have heard, whilst in New Zealand, th[e] institution of this bureau assaile[d] as Socialistic by the opponen[ts] of the Government, but wheth[er] the charge they also make that [it] is used as a means of politic[al]

positive in denying it. It is to be hoped that such cha
perfectly groundless, for if there is one thing more cert
another, it is that if the Labour Party are to main
present hold they have on the confidence of the peopl
only be by the conduct of government on the lines of pu
integrity.

Amongst other measures of the present Government
for the protection of the native birds, animals, and p
New Zealand, and for this purpose an island is to be pu
and set apart as a sort of native Zoological and Botanical
Undoubtedly this is a most useful measure, and clearl
that a Labour Government is not unmindful of the c
science. Another useful act is the Shop Assistants'
regulating the hours of shop assistants. These an
measures passed by the present Government tend to pr
it is a competent, capable, and sound Government, a
that the fears of those who are alarmed for the futur
English race, because of the probability that there will l
future a greater share of political power in the hands
Labour Party than has been wielded by them in the p
utterly without foundation. If these nervous peopl
only carefully study history, they would come to the co
that just as all the revolutions the world has ever se
been brought about by the accumulation of wealth in th
of the few, accompanied by the political serfdom of the
so the best guarantee for the progress, developme
prosperity of a nation, is only to be found in the gra
full political power and liberty to the people, than w
portion of a nation sooner feel the effects of good
legislation; and, consequently, than whom no porti
nation can be so safely relied on to uphold the one and a
other.

I would not have it thought to be my opinion th
is any form of government that can be devised that wil
from faults and imperfections. I have not the slighte
that had I stayed longer in New Zealand I should ha

that considering this is the first opportunity the Labour Party have had of using their power, they have used it with singular moderation, and have shown the desire and capacity to govern wisely and in a statesmanlike manner. But whatever has been the result in New Zealand, or whatever may be the result there in the future, will not alter the principle that the only safe Government is that which rests on the people, and in which every class of which the nation is composed are fairly and impartially represented.

We spent New Year's Day at sea on our voyage from New Zealand to Melbourne, via Tasmania. It is wonderful how such an occasion will draw all the passengers together cementing old friendships and making new ones. We thought of all our friends at home and tried to imagine exactly what they would be doing. Altogether, New Year's day at sea has a solemnity and impressiveness which one never realises on land.

We arrived at Hobart, Tasmania, at noon on Bank Holiday January 2nd, and a beautiful day it was, bright and clear, the hot sun tempered with cool breezes. We found the city itself entirely deserted, for if there is one thing more dear to the heart of a Colonial than another it is a holiday; and especially so on that holiday there are races, cricket matches, yachting, other sports to be seen. In love of sport they are even more English than the English. And their beautiful climate, which allows everyone to wear light dresses without fear of the consequences, and the absence of any of those signs of poverty and wretchedness which we unfortunately meet with on such occasions at home, combine to produce a picture that can never be forgotten, and make a general holiday in Australia one of the happiest sights imaginable. We left Hobart just as the holiday makers were returning, and enjoyed a fine moonlight sail down the harbour, arriving in Melbourne the Wednesday following.

AUSTRALIA.

A STRANGER visiting Sydney is sure to be asked on[e ques]tion, "Have you seen our harbour?" Although w[e were] asked scores of other questions in Melbourne, no one all[uded to] the harbour, but as if to make up for their shortcomings

FAIRY BOWER, MANLY.

respect—for their harbour is merely a canal, like the C[lyde at] Glasgow—Melbourne itself is one of the finest cities [in the] world. Built on the American plan, with broad straight s[treets] crossing each other at right angles, and with lofty, many-s[toreyed]

were all built with borrowed money at a time when the surplus capital of England was literally forced on the Colonies, it is quite clear that the question of expense had no place in the calculations of those who designed them. We could not help recalling the many shabby public buildings we have at home and regretting that some portion of this " surplus capital " was not devoted to providing us with buildings that would be more worthy of our large cities and enable them to take their proper place amongst the cities of the world. Any third-rate town or city on the Continent, or in America, or in the Colonies, in this respect, could put to the blush our cities at home. It appears to me that we are just as much behind the age in public buildings as our Colonies are in advance, and I say in advance because it does not appear sound for a young nation to go to unnecessary and luxurious expense in buildings, until the same can be done without resorting to loans. It is impossible to visit Melbourne without admiring the completeness of the cable tramway system there—which is produced by private enterprise—nor without comparing it with the Government tramways at Sydney which are probably the worst the world can show. But it is not only in the plan of the city, the width and straightness of its streets and tramway system, that Melbourne approaches the American models, but also in a thousand other details. You cannot please a Melbourne man more than to say how American everything is. Sydney, on the other hand, is a thoroughly English city, reminding one of a blend of Manchester and Liverpool, and the Sydneyite prides himself on being English to the backbone, claiming that the business done in his city is more solid and settled than the business of Melbourne. Certainly, Sydney during the last few years has made more progress than Melbourne in commerce, and is to-day securing a greater proportion of the trade of all Australasia.

AUSTRALIAN DAIRY FARMING.

IN one respect Victoria at the present time is in adv[ance of] New South Wales, and that is in the dairy indus[try—the] shipment of butter to England. Whilst we were in Vict[oria we] visited a butter factory, and we also visited one in New [South] Wales. Both are conducted on exactly the same system [. In] Victoria there are many such factories, and the industry [is well] established, whilst in New South Wales there are fe[w, and] the industry is in its infancy. The following is, as ne[arly as I] can describe it, the system adopted in butter facto[ries in] Australia. The system is founded on a right knowl[edge of] the laws that govern economical and skilful productio[n in all] industries—division of labour. Just as the man who [grows] cotton does not attempt to manufacture it into cali[co, but] devotes all his energy to the growth of cotton alo[ne, so] under the modern factory system of butter maki[ng the] farmer who produces the milk does not make it into but[ter, but] devotes all his energy to producing more milk. The [butter] factory itself is generally placed in some large town or c[ity, and] has in connection with it a number of small creameries s[cattered] through the country districts, each fitted up with the [latest] centrifugal separators for extracting the cream from th[e milk.] The butter factory does not want the skim milk. It only [wants] the cream. Therefore it buys only the cream from the [farmer,] paying him at the rate of threepence to fourpence for the [cream] contained in one gallon of milk, the farmer retaining th[e skim] milk for feeding purposes. The milk is tested, and if no[t of the] normal standard a corresponding reduction in payment is [made.] These creameries are conducted at very small expens[e, and] therefore each factory has a great number of them, conv[eniently]

any required temperature, as can also the dairy where th
butter is made, worked, and finally packed for shipment.
the churn room are a number of churns, each capable
producing 800lbs. of butter in from twenty to thirty minut
From the churns the butter is taken to an adjoining roor
where it is properly worked, salted, and packed, but during a
these processes it is not once touched by hand. We all kno
the importance of an even temperature if butter of one unifor
good quality is to be produced. To ensure this the dairy
provided with a heating apparatus, consisting of hot wat
pipes, for use in winter, by the aid of which, and of the col
air engine in summer, the temperature never varies the ye
round. The factory we saw in Victoria can produce 112,000lb
of butter each week, and the owners will guarantee every pour
to be of exactly the same quality. I suppose, roughly speakin
this quantity of butter represents the produce of 15,000
20,000 cows, or, allowing an average of 30 cows to each far
the produce of from 500 to 650 farms. And now we see t
twofold advantage of this system, for it is clear that, owing
variation in temperature, if each farmer made his own milk in
butter, it could not be so good in quality as the butter ma
with the aid of the modern appliances at the factory, and,
addition, there would be no two farmers with quality alike, a
secondly, the labour required to make the butter at over 5
farms would be incomparably greater than the labour at o
central factory, aided by steam power, etc. In consequence t
system is a thorough success.

It would appear that the English farmer ought to find th
system equally profitable in England. In the first place, I
would save the serious expense of one penny per pound, t
cost of freight on the Australian butter home. In addition, I
butter, lightly salted and quite fresh, would command at lea
twopence per pound over the Australian butter, which is abo
two months old before it can reach the consumer. Might n
dairy farming on these lines be further developed in Englanc
Of course all land at home is not suitable for dairy purposes, b
it is equally true that all the land that is suitable is not so use

are not in a position to judge what dairy farming in Engla
become. In Australia dairy farm land is almost as dear,
quite as dear, when near the cities, as the same class of
England, and yet, in Australia, even at the extremely low
realized for the cream, dairying is viewed as the most pro
of all farming. I ought not to forget to mention th
Government in Australia takes what some would be incl
call a paternal interest in agriculture and dairying.
Government expense, lecturers travel through country di
instructing the farmers how to make the best of their lan
most suitable crops for them to cultivate; and also the r
methods of dairying. Many people do not believe
expense being thrown on the public, call it "grandmot
and declare that it would be just as proper to send ro
teach the village blacksmith his business at the public ex
Undoubtedly, there is much truth in this. But at the
time it is quite clear that if the blacksmith did not unde
his business, or was behindhand in modern methods of
shoeing, it would be a thousand times better for the publi
experts should be sent at Government expense to tead
than to have all the horses in the country only able to
the work they were capable of if shod according to the
modern methods. I must not omit to mention that the
which the Victorian Government have hitherto given on
exported, ceases this winter. It was a pernicious system
is certain that the money paid as bonus never got furthe
the pockets of the exporters. The price the farmer got
cream has been unaffected by it. His price is the same i
South Wales, where no bonus has ever been given, as
Victoria, where the bonus has been given.

Probably the dearest item of living in Australia is hous
To anyone fresh from the old country the rents asked
cities and towns of Australia are simply astounding. A w
man's cottage, with three bedrooms, would be hard to
Sydney at less than 13s. to 15s. per week, and with a p
20s. a week would be the rent asked. Small semi-de

rate of wages is one shilling per hour who cannot average mo
than 20s. per week, and judging from all I could learn, I do n
think that, taking all Australia, the condition of the workin
man is superior to that of his brother at home. And it is cle
that the seemingly high rate of wages and the irregular nature
most of the employment have a decidedly demoralising effect o
those engaged in such work. Take wool shearers, for instance
for two months these men can make £6 to £9 per week b
working at what, for want of a better word, I must ca
"concert pitch." Then it is all over, and as a result of th
strain, and being flush with cash, they naturally spend son
portion, perhaps in some cases even all, of their earnings
drink; so that, after deducting their expenses to and from th
sheep runs, there is little left to keep wife and family on, and con
sequently they have to depend on anything that may turn up t
find them work for the rest of the year. The same, only in
less degree, now applies to stonemasons, joiners, etc. Th
wages are higher than in England, but work is not steady, and
gather that at the present time many have not had employmer
for some months. In fact, deputations have lately waited on th
Government demanding that fresh public buildings be con
menced to find them employment. The only reply the Govern
ment could make was that it was impossible to borrow th
necessary money. Had they been able to do so, fresh publi
buildings would, no doubt, have been commenced, not becaus
they were required for the business of the country, but to main
tain an unnatural state of affairs—a rate of wages the countr
cannot afford to give. I do not, therefore, consider the positio
of the workman in Australia superior to that of his brother a
home, but distinctly inferior. Protection, which makes most o
the necessaries of life dear, and the high rents which must b
met every week, are heavy handicaps in life's race. If a man i
out of work he may live on little food, he may put off buyin
clothing and many other expenses, but he cannot put off ren
day, and if the rent is high, most of his wages, when he is agai
in work, will have to go to the landlord.

But it is not only house rents that are high. Shop and offic

England is one of great difficulty, but in Australia it is e⋯
worse. In the Colonies a small man has not sufficient t⋯
to buy well, so even if he had the capital he cannot imp⋯
own goods, and, therefore, cannot compete with larger m⋯
are able to do this. Of course, large buyers always h⋯
advantage over smaller ones, but what I wish to make ⋯
that the advantages reaped by the former in Australia ⋯
much greater than is the case at home, that small buye⋯
are in a very much worse position than small buyers a⋯
There is no room for a man with a little capital to start ⋯
ness in Australia. He will do infinitely better at hom⋯
only class there is an opening for in the Colonies at the ⋯
time are men with a little capital and some knowl⋯
farming. These will do much better in the Colonies ⋯
home; and no other class will. Clerks and profession⋯
are probably as a whole greater sufferers in the Coloni⋯
any other class.

SYDNEY AND BRISBANE.

WHAT a lovely harbour Sydney possesses, and how justl[y] proud the Sydneyites are of it! You are sure to be aske[d] by everyone you meet this one question, "Have you seen o[ur] harbour?" This gets a little monotonous after, say, the on[e] hundredth repetition, and finally, in desperation, you go to se[e] the harbour, perhaps even arrange to devote a whole day [to] seeing it. You are astonished at its beauty, and still mo[re]

LAVENDER BAY AND SYDNEY.

astonished to find that you could not explore the whole of it

and wooded to the water's edge. Here are peaceful beaches, there steep precipitous rocks, whilst dotted ab beautiful wooded islets. At no point do the opposite appear more than two or three miles away, and in mos not more than one mile. The villas and houses, amongst the trees and along the shores, make one envy of the happy mortals who have found such delightful s their homes. There is one drawback, however, from bather's point of view—this peaceful harbour, looking and still, is the happy hunting ground of the shark, suspecting bathing parties are occasionally raided by "man eater," with fatal results. From the yachtsman's view, another drawback is that sudden gusts of wi descend on his craft, and if the spreading canvas ca quickly lowered, all that the most skilful can do will n to save him. But there is "no rose without a thorr some drawbacks one must expect to find in every favoui the world over. At home we have our grumble at the Out in Sydney such a thing is impossible. Therefor Nature, knowing that humanity can never be truly happ out something to grumble at, thoughtfully provid grievance.

The Australian climate appears to approach very n the ideal. I must confess that before we landed there been rather alarmed by accounts of the thermometer reg 123 degrees in the shade, but—and we suppose our exper the average one—we never saw the thermometer in th rise above on one occasion 95 degrees, on two or three o 90 degrees, and, perhaps, on half a dozen occasions, 85 During all the rest of our stay in Australia the therm varied from 75 to 80 degrees. The air is so fresh and that, with cool clothing, this temperature is rather agreea otherwise. But, then, our friends told us we were e> lucky in the weather. We must admit that we were s our visit to Brisbane, for, if all accounts are true, we have had a warm reception there. A story was told us c

to implore to be allowed to take back a few blankets. "It was
so cold down there." Probably this story is not founded on fac
—it may only have been circulated by other cities, jealous of the
success of Brisbane, just as certain cities talk about the coldness
of Toronto
and Montreal.
The man who
told us, how-
ever, said he
knew a man
who knew a
man who had
seen the bro-
ther of the

VICTORIA BRIDGE,
BRISBANE.

H.M.S. "KATOOMBA," OFF BRISBANE.

dead man—
therefore
give it as i
was told us
and to shov
that we ha
every reaso
to expect i
to be hot a
Brisbane
Even as we went up in the train we read accounts in the paper
that they were having the hottest week known in Brisbane fo
many years; that the thermometer registered 115 degrees in th
shade, and 147 degrees in the sun. Well, the very night w
landed in Brisbane, the heat, which had lasted without a breal

cold it was and how very liable people were to take a c
cold weather. Now when one meets with people whc
degrees in the shade cold and chilly, it is only reaso
suppose they are accustomed to something hotter. Tl
our experience as to Australia having an ideal climate
an exaggerated one. We hoped we had at least found
in the world where the clerk of the weather attende
duties properly, and where he produced the very best a
his line this world is capable of.

AUSTRALIA AND ONE MAN ONE VOTE.

I MUST not forget to mention a subject that just now is engaging public attention in New South Wales, especially as the same question will shortly be before our own Parliament at home, and that is "One man one vote." The Lower House having passed a bill providing for this, it has now to be dealt with by the Upper House. In that august assembly it has had the effect of producing a great deal of solicitude and fear that the passing of such a bill would discourage the practise of thrift in the colony. The Upper House professes to agree entirely with the principle of "one man one vote." but says that to make it law would have the effect of discouraging "thrift," since by such a bill, the man who possesses no property, houses, or land—the man with "no stake in the country." nothing, in fact, but his manhood,—would have just the same vote as the man who by thrift had acquired some share of this world's goods. "This, says the Upper House, " must necessarily discourage the thrifty man, which is not a wise thing to do. On the contrary, he ought to be encouraged to a still greater practice of thrift, by giving him an extra vote for the possession of that virtue." We know we are only a slow-going lot at home, otherwise we should be at a loss to tell how it is that our social reformers have been so behind the age as not to have made the discovery of how great a power for good may be made of that much abused custodian of our liberties—the Ballot Box. But, now that the discovery has been given to the world, surely such an enormous power for good will not be confined to the Colonies. Let England enjoy her share of the blessing. Now that we

sobriety, we must give a vote for sobriety; bravery, v give a vote for bravery; unselfishness, we must give a v unselfishness; honesty, we must give a vote for h truthfulness, we must give a vote for truthfulness; w give a vote for each virtue taught and preached by our S we must give a vote for the keeping of each of t Commandments. It would be little less than a crim blessings of this beautiful and simple system were conf the encouragement of only one solitary virtue; and espec when that is a virtue which many think is not even on most exalted for man to aspire to. A man might practis in the very highest degree without being remarkable possession of any other virtue; nay, he might even lack the other virtues, and yet not be seriously handicappe practice of thrift. A man might lead a useful and blame and practice thrift in order to feed, clothe, and educ family, or in order to support father, mother, or sick rel and because, whilst practising thrift, he practised also virtue, the law of Christ, "Bear ye one another's burde might never have that outward show of thrift—the guinea stamp for it—the ownership of property.

We all know that even now the lot of the revising b is not a happy one, especially when, say, the agents of t political parties are fighting like two dogs for a bone knotty point in some lodger's claim for a vote. But it is bed of roses compared to what it would be had he to de claims for "votes for thrift." Just fancy the eviden would be hunted up to support the claims brought forw energetic secretaries, Liberal and Conservative. I reme rich man whose will, when he died, was sworn at ov millions sterling, who once in a mad fit of generosity—h not to be too severely blamed for this, such a thing occurr seldom—gave his cowman a worn-out pair of boots. W few days' time the rich man again saw his cowman, he wa I won't say surprised, because that does not half exp feelings. I had better say dumbfounded, to notice that th

I have done with them." There would be no resisting such evidence as the above in support of a claim for a "vote for thrift." In fact, it ought to win two votes, one for the master and one for the man, and then fancy the haul it would be to the party which secured such interesting evidence.

We can imagine the result of the evidence, say in the next case, that of a man who had brought up a large family on small wages, and who, though he had never missed a day's work in his life, and although his wife had darned and turned, hemmed and stitched the clothes of the family, yet had never succeeded in doing more than keep out of debt, after the landlord had had his rent and he himself a "pipe of 'bacca." Such evidence as this would never get a vote for thrift. The revising barrister would point out with great force and logic that the "pipe of 'bacca" was fatal to the claim; and however much he regretted it under the circumstances, he had no other course than to disallow the vote.

Of course all this time I am supposing that the claim to a vote for thrift would be settled on evidence of thrift, but I must confess there is no foundation for this supposition. I rather gathered from what I heard in New South Wales, that in proposing a vote for thrift, it was not intended to make it necessary to have any very deep inquiry into the practice of that virtue. It was simply proposed to settle the right to a vote for thrift on evidence of ownership of property. If a man had property, he would get his vote for thrift, though he were the greatest spendthrift that ever wasted a fortune. If he had no property, then he would get no vote for thrift, though he were the very embodiment of that virtue. In short, the so-called vote for thrift is only a colonial development of the old Tory dodge tersely described by Mr. Gladstone as "deck loading." The Upper House, knowing it dare not refuse passage to the good ship, "one man one vote," hopes that by deck loading her with a so-called "vote for thrift," it may either sink the ship or deprive the owners of any profit should she reach port in safety.

It is strange to notice what a strong family likeness there is

appear to be impressed with the one idea—that they exist
to maintain the power and influence of property on a
altogether out of proportion to what property is fairly e
to; that they must stand through all eternity, a faithfu
pledged to keep back the rising tide of democracy, or
like heroes in the attempt. They cannot see that such me
as "one man one vote, the transferring of power from t
to the many, are merely the natural outcome and devel
of the growth of intellect in the nation, brought ab
educational facilities and a cheap and free press. They ce
do not realize the true position, which is, that thos
advocate such measures as "one man one vote," are fight
the side of law and order and of constitutional gover
whilst those who oppose such measures are doing all that
their power to make a way for the anarchist and commun

AUSTRALIA AND FREE TRADE.

IF I have had very little to say about the natural wonde[rs] and beauties of Australia, it must not be supposed th[at] Australia is not rich in these, but merely that it was [o]ur misfortune not to be able to visit them. The fact is that all o[ur] time in Australia was spent in the cities and towns. The wonders of the Blue Mountains, of the Janolan Caves, and of bush life, are all unknown to us We did hope that at least we should see the kangaroo on his "native heather," but the only kangaroos we saw were some dejected looking specimens in the Adelaide Zoological Gardens. We did not see half a dozen rabbits in all Australia, and yet we must believe the statement that there are millions there. We are quite willing to

something Australian to take home, we were reduced
necessity of buying at a shop in Sydney a stuffed specimen
animal—the ornithorincus—or some such name it is kn
The name is curious enough, but the animal is still m
because it combines with the bill of a duck, the fur of
the flesh and skeleton of a reptile, lays eggs like a hen,
suckles its young like the familiar cat. It is clear, as
can see after such a description as this, that our friends
would be quite justified in believing we had the specimen
order, like Barnum's mermaid, and as we have never s
animal in its native lair, why of course we can only refe
shopman—a very weak and ridiculous position for trave
have to take up, and one for which there is no preceden
same with regard to the native Blackfellow and his gin
Our knowledge of them and of their boomerang and
throwing feats is limited to the Saturday afternoon perfo
of a tribe in the grounds of the old Melbourne Exhibitio
even this performance will probably be just as well seer
Royal Aquarium, London, in a few months time. Of co
may be argued that this is, after all, the most comfortal
to see them. That to journey hundreds of miles up c
sleeping at night by the camp fire on which we had just
our supper of "dampers," and boiled our "billy" of tea
if anything but an ostrich could sleep after such a supper
very well, but one might find it a little too "roughing it
being accustomed to hotels with elevators and call-boys

But if we could not enjoy the pleasures of a trip up th
we can the better indulge in one pleasure dearest of
the heart of a globe trotter. And in indulging without
this pleasure, the fact that I was only three or four w
Australia need not be allowed to restrain me in the sl
Nay, the shorter the globe trotter's stay in a coun
more charms this pleasure has for him, because
acquaintance with the country, by increasing his kno
would undoubtedly shatter many of his pet schem
theories; and if his knowledge of the country wer

knows, is to point out some of the shortcomings of the country and the way to put everything to rights.

Being a Free Trader, naturally the first thing that strikes me a huge blunder in the colonies is the policy of Protection they have adopted. The next is the working man's phase of Protection—a desire to discourage immigration. These two naturally go together, and the one is just as wise and just as reasonable as the other. Then, of course, the way the land has been dealt with is a big mistake. How could it be otherwise, when the pioneer law makers had only the English model to go by? Railways, from the question of gauges up to the system of rates and charges, are worked on a wrong system. And as to the finances, they speak for themselves, and he must be a very po specimen of the globe trotter who could not tell Australia about that.

AUSTRALIAN VENUS.

If a man is at all shaky in his views on Free Trade, let hi visit Protectionist countries. I know of nothing that will soon convince him that Free Trade is not only the best for the worl but also the best for the country that adopts it, even with

brothers in the countries I have named. And the curious
is, the Protectionist does not know what more he can do
matters right without approaching to Free Trade. For
when it was possible to argue that duties were not high e
it was thought that it was only necessary to increase tl
rectify any evil. Now, when duties can no longer be inc
without their becoming not Protection but Prohibition, n
are as far off being right as ever. Take the woollen indu
Victoria, for instance. One would expect that as the v
raised at the very door of the mill, whilst the Bradfo
Continental manufacturers must be put to heavy exper
carriage, woollen manufacture would be a native indu
Victoria. But it is not so. To quote from the Melbourne
Mr. Deakin, a Protectionist member of the Victoria Parli
said, in a speech in the House. "This woollen industry pre
more problems to him, as a Protectionist, than any other
colony. This industry, which ought to be a success, whi
natural, if any industry was natural, in which they ought
their mills not only readily commanding the local mark
also invading outside markets, was continually before ther
the sickly complaint of need of support. The problem wa
these mills were not a success, which, according to his t
they ought to be, and why they needed this continua
creasing measure of Protection." We have always hear
in protected industries the wages of the working man were
—in fact, good wages to the workman are promised as t
off against the certainty that he will have to pay more
commodities he buys. And yet this is what Mr. Dea
Protectionist, mind, says in the same speech, "the wages
this industry (woollen). were not in proportion to the intell
of the employees, or the hours they worked."

But even the Protectionists themselves do not dare
Protection at a time when the credit of their country is at
One would expect that, at a time when things were in
way, then would be just the opportunity Protectionists
long for, in order to show the virtues of their method. A
hear what the Premier of New South Wales—Sir George

views on the necessity for a Protective tariff **far more** stringer
than at present, but they held it to be their first duty to restor
the credit of the colony." Why, this is the very thing the Pro
tectionists claim that Protection will do. But they know
would do **no such thing,** and being really alarmed at the **state o**
affairs, they prefer a Free Trade income tax "to restore th
credit of the colony," **after** which they **will try** more stringer
Protection than ever—if the credit of the **colony is** robust **enoug**
to stand it.

The Melbourne *Argus* gave a collection **of the sayings o**
Protectionists in the Colonies. from which **I take the following** :-

"That infant industries need Protection, **but the** older th
infant industries grow, **the more** Protection **they** require
"**That** taxing an article makes it cheaper." "That making a
article cheaper enables the manufacturer to pay higher wages t
his workmen." "That inter-colonial Free Trade **is a necessity**
but it would be grossly unfair **not** to tax products coming fror
the sister states." "**That to** raise **revenue** from customs, yo
should impose duties **that** would stop importations." "Tha
Protection lowers prices, but that farmers are entitled to con
pensation for **having** to pay more for (protected) commodities.
"That Protection **destroys** the importers' **monopoly, which i**
good, and will give **the** manufacturer **a** monopoly, **which i**
better."

A curious incident occurred in Victoria, over duties impose
by a provisional bill—**on** the strength of which the duties wer
collected—whereas the bill was finally rejected. The questio
then arose as to refunding the duty paid. The very sam
member who had stated when the bill was under discussion tha
the duties would not increase prices, because they would be pai
by the importer **and not by** the consumer, when the bill wa
afterwards rejected, opposed the duties being refunded to th
importer, on the grounds that he had not actually paid them
but had charged them on **to the** retailer, who had charged ther
to the consumer. **These two** speeches were made within fiv
days of each other. But a grocer told me the most amusing
story. One of his customers, **a** Protectionist, complained tha

the importer paid the duties, and not us." After a lot of
the grocer convinced his customer that, notwithstandi[ng]
the member said, this could not be so showed him w[hat]
goods cost and what the duty amounted to, and finally
the man that importers could not pay the duties. "[No]
more Protection for me," said the customer, as he left.

You would expect that Protectionists everywhere w[ere]
disappointed at the victory of Cleveland as a blow to thei[r.]
But it is not so. Australia would gladly see Americ[an]
Free Trade to-morrow. I have never met in all my t[ime a]
Protectionist living outside England who wished to see [Protec-]
tion established in England, or anywhere else for that [matter]
beyond the frontiers of his own country. This is so con[trary to]
what is usual with the champions and supporters of a[ny]
cause, that it clearly shows the hollowness of the claim [that any]
man, or body of men, believe in Protection. No m[an can]
believe in Protection, although there are thoroughly ho[nest men]
who think they do. But if they carefully analysed the [basis of]
their own belief, they would find that it rested not on [the fact]
that Protection is good in itself, but on the shoals and quic[ksands]
that Protection appears likely to put money int[o their]
own pockets. So far as the manufacturers and work[men are]
concerned, this ultimately proves to be a complete fallac[y. The]
history of protected industries shows industries that ha[ve]
started in the colonies under the wing of protected tarif[fs have]
shown the most wonderful capacity for losing mone[y. The]
consequence is that Protectionists, finding their protecte[d manu-]
factures a failure, cry out for inter-colonial Free Trade, [which is]
a step, even if a small step, nearer to Free Trade. Wh[en they]
get this, their protected industries will still be in the m[ire, and]
they will cry out—some are doing so already—for Fre[e Trade]
with Great Britain, with some sort of Protection against [the rest]
of the world. This would be another step away from Pr[otection]
and towards Free Trade. But, mind, it is not the Free [Traders]
who ask for this step to be taken, but the Protectioni[sts.]
Free Trade kills commercially local manufacturers, will t[hey]

get a step nearer Free Trade, as if it represented the flesh pots of Egypt, is a contradiction to the doctrine of Protection. "'Tis a mad world, my masters," and of all mad worlds the Protectionists' world is the maddest.

It is only natural that since the manufacturers get Protection the farmer and workman should look for a certain measure of Protection also. This takes the form not exactly of prohibiting the immigration of competing farmers and workmen, but of preventing the Government from taking any steps to facilitate immigration. The farmer and workman will not allow State aided immigration, which they think would interfere with their interests. Any Government that brought out such a scheme would be certain to meet with defeat, and yet some such scheme is most urgently required for the opening up of the colonies. And this opposition is bound to exist as long as Protection is the policy of the country. It cannot be otherwise. Do away with the one and the other will die a natural death, and then will follow the rapid development of the colonies and increased prosperity for all.

AUSTRALIA AND THE LAND QUESTIO

"WATER, water, everywhere, and not a drop to dri
we read this, "Land, land, everywhere, and no
to till," it would hardly be any exaggeration of the positio
land question in Australia. For the land available for the
at a reasonable price and of good quality is not rightly situ:
the markets, and the land that is right for the markets
good quality is firmly held by speculators for a rise, a
prices they ask for what little they are willing from time
to sell, make it dearer when cleared, fenced, and provid

A SETTLER'S HUT.

buildings, than would be the price of similar land in E
The manner in which the land of the country has bee
with in the early history of the colonies, and the way ir
it has passed out of the hands of the people without any
ponding advantage to the State, is one of the greatest hinc

of one pound per acre. Having acquired millions of acres
these easy terms, the owners "sit down" and wait the develo[p]
ment of the surrounding country to reap their "unearn[ed]
increment." Take the case of one well-known English-Aust[ra]
lian Land Company. In the early years of Australian coloni[sa]
tion they acquired over one million acres of the best land on t[he]
above easy terms. Coal was afterwards discovered, both und[er]
their land and also under adjoining land, which they did not ow[n.]
Not satisfied with this lucky find, for which they had not p[aid]
one farthing, they actually tried to stop the coal being work[ed]
on the adjoining land, claiming that their deeds gave them t[he]
sole right to get coal in that colony. Of course the cou[rt]
decided against them, and their monopoly was broken u[p.]
Everyone can see that had they succeeded in making good th[eir]
monstrous claim, it would have stifled the manufacturing a[nd]
other industries on which the progress of the colony depen[ds,]
but everyone cannot so readily see that the ownership, or, [in]
other words, monopoly of one million acres of land by one m[an]
or company is, equally, morally wrong, and equally against t[he]
progress of the colony. But this is so, as is shown by its eff[ect]
on the colony as a whole, and on the town that has sprung up [in]
that neighbourhood. The town is growing all on one si[de,]
extending on the adjoining land that is uncontrolled by the La[nd]
Company, because the Land Company hold for extreme price[s.]
Their land, having cost nothing, does not eat itself up in intere[st]
and therefore they can afford to do this. Some years back t[he]
town wished to acquire a few acres of the Company's land f[or]
the purposes of a recreation ground, when the price asked th[em]
was £1,000 per acre. This raised such a hue and cry, th[at,]
alarmed for the consequences, the Company, with as good gra[ce]
as they could assume, at short notice, elected to make the to[wn]
a present of the land.

What is the consequence of this abominable state of affair[s?]
Within a radius of 100 miles of Sydney, there is not an acre [of]
land that the settler could buy at its fair honest value, and ther[e]
fore the settler has to take "back blocks," whence to get h[is]

There was a time, no doubt, when owners would ha[ve]
considered to be well within their rights in dealing wi[th]
land in any way they thought best in their own intere[st,]
there are unmistakeable signs that this is no longer t[he]
Property has its rights, but it also has its duties, a[nd]
neglects the latter it has no claim to the enjoyment [of]
former. No man can now claim the right to "do what [he]
with his own." The law has stepped in, in a thousand i[nstances]
and exploded that doctrine so morally wrong. And it [will]
be a short time longer before right judgment will prev[ail in]
regard to this burning evil of ownership of land by those [who]
not put it to its best uses. When that day comes t[he]
owner will be told, "We recognise the rights you hav[e in the]
land you possess, but there is a greater right even tha[t,]
and that is the right of the people to access to the [land on]
equitable terms, that they may put the land to the best [use it is]
capable of, and find employment for themselves an[d their]
children. To secure this in future, our land taxation w[ill be so]
graduated that whilst it falls very lightly on those whos[e land is]
put to proper uses, it will fall with crushing force o[n the]
holders of big estates whose land is not being put to [its best]
uses. It shall be as extravagant a luxury to ho[ld land]
negligently as it is to keep a yacht or a stud of hunters[, and as]
profitable to hold land that is put to its best uses as it i[s to own]
a ship or a team of wagon horses."

AUSTRALIAN RAILWAYS AND FINANCE.

A STRANGER arriving at Melbourne and wishing to go to Sydney would be astonished to find that **before he** could pass into New South Wales he would be compelled, **no matter** what hour of the day or night, to change carriages, **simply** because **there is a** 5ft. 3in. gauge **in** Victoria, and a 4ft. 8½in. gauge in New South Wales. In Queensland again the gauge is 3ft. 6in. and in South Australia 5ft. 3in. If you ask a Melbourne man why this is so, he answers, " Oh, that is the confounded **jealousy** of the Sydney people. We had our railways **first, why could not they take** the **same gauge?** It was **not likely we would** alter to suit **them."** If you **ask a Sydney** man **he says,** " The Melbourne gauge is all **wrong.** Our gauge is the gauge of the world. It is just like Melbourne to take something different to all the rest of the world **and then expect us to follow.** We are **right, they are wrong." The fact is no one can realize the** jealousy between the Australian colonies **who has not visited** them. However **this** jealousy is not so great to-day **as it** used to be, and there **are** signs that it will soon be **a** thing of **the** past.

But if the gauges on the Australian railways **are bad the** rates and charges are worse. They seem **to** have been specially designed to discourage the use of railways as much as possible. The following, from the **Year** Book of **New** South Wales, 1893 will give some idea of railway rates. "**The** maximum rate for any class **of** merchandise (except explosives) from Sydney to Bourke (500 **miles)** will be £41 per **truck load not** exceeding six **tons.** A rebate of £3 per **truck on** general merchandise, and £6 **per truck on** sugar, rice, unwrought and galvanised iron, etc. Smaller quantities at the ordinary mileage rates." Such rates must simply **kill any farming** industry **up country.** A Sydney **broker** told me **that it is** not unusual for **up-country** sheep, sent

of carriage and expenses. Now the object of railways
huge continent like Australia, as elsewhere, is to ann
distance so as to connect all parts of the country wi
centres of population. And it is clear that, where the ra
belong to the people themselves, it is directly against
interests to make railway rates so high that a monopoly is
to those who, by their situation as regards the market
protected from competition with those whose produce ca
be brought to market by payment of heavy railway rates.
high rates on their railways, the Government become par
a monopoly. This is not the system on which Gover
railway rates ought to be based. There is only one w
make the railways pay the nation properly, and at the
time place every part of the country on an equal footing
that is to annihilate distance in fixing rates. Just as t
one uniform rate for postage and telegrams within a kin
regardless of distance, so there ought to be one unifor
per ton for carriage on the railways and one uniform r
passengers, regardless of distance. It will all work ou
on the basis of the average carriage per ton, and the a
fare per passenger. This is shown, in a smaller way, b
experience in letter postage, telegrams, and parcels pos
present the expense on the long distance trains is n
distance, but the few passengers who travel long dist
And so with goods, it is not the haulage of a greater
number of miles that is costly, but the terminal charges.
experience of the parcels post in this matter is a guid
7-pound parcel costs a shilling to send to the next town, s
miles away, and it only costs the same to send it to the fu
corner of the kingdom, say 500 miles away. But becau
this, everyone does not send parcels 500 miles only—the
send them wherever their destination is, regardless of dis
with the result that the system proves a sound one. To b
position to work railways on such a system as this, tha
say, in the same way that Government now works the
and telegraph service, appears to me to be the only adva

AUSTRALIAN RAILWAYS AND FINANCE. 1

Government to bear the loss on the foreign cable and r
services. At present the heavy railway rates press entirely
the struggling up country settler and crush him almost ou
existence. If there were any loss, which could only be in
initiation of the system, it would fall with lightness on
whole nation, who would gain more than they lost thereby
they would have command of every market and centre
production and distribution in the kingdom, and break
monopoly in any one district.

During our visit to Australia the all absorbing question
the newspapers was the finances of the Colonies. I do not t
a gloomy view of the financial position of the Colonies. T
indebtedness certainly looks at first sight heavy, but in realit
is not so. The only fair way to view the matter is to consider,
how much do the Colonies owe, but what they have got to sl
for it. And viewed in this light, if properly marketed, their r
ways, tramways, waterworks, and other productive wo
alone, would, I am informed, realize close upon, if not fully,
total amount of their debts. But there is one respect in wl
the Colonies are not sound, and that is the extravagance
their expenditure. Every succeeding Government pledges it
to reduce expenditure, and just as certainly ends by increas
it. No government has yet been found strong enough to ca
out a policy of retrenchment. Whilst we were in Sydney a
of repentance and economy was in full operation, the Gove
ment of New South Wales said they were determined to m
ends meet, and proposed both to put on an Income Tax a
to reduce expenses. Immediately an indignant member rise
the House and declares that if the Government cuts down
vote for roads and bridges and other matters in the district
represents, he shall withdraw his support. And so it g
merrily on. Everyone has his own axe to grind and his c
relatives or friends to find a snug billet for, and whilst all
agreed that the expenditure must be reduced, no Governm
seems to have the power to carry it out. But such matters
these have a way of settling themselves, and in the pres
instance this is being brought about by the withdrawal of cre

legitimate requirement. It is one of the characteristics o to find a difficulty in living within its income, and Aus merely suffering from this experience now. Of her fi soundness and of her powers to grow out of this phase youth there can be no doubt in the mind of any person w visited the country. Nor can there be any doubt of th future time has in store for her. As Englishmen, we hav reason to feel proud that the large and powerful nation growing up in Australia sprang from our own country, our own language, and is connected with us in the closes of brotherhood. The Australians always speak of Great as "Home," or the "Old Country," but oftenest as " I and the bond that exists between us is one of love and af the result of the recognition by the parent of the right offspring to self-government, and of the esteem and reg the parent which this has engendered in the offspring.

www.ingramcontent.com/pod-product-compliance
Lightning Source LLC
Chambersburg PA
CBHW022131160426
43197CB00009B/1242